THANKSGIVING

Thanksgiving

THE HOLIDAY AT THE HEART
OF THE AMERICAN EXPERIENCE

MELANIE KIRKPATRICK

ENCOUNTER BOOKS NEW YORK ★ LONDON

© 2016 by Melanie Kirkpatrick

First American edition published in 2016 by Encounter Books,
an activity of Encounter for Culture and Education, Inc.,
a nonprofit, tax exempt corporation.
Encounter Books website address: www.encounterbooks.com

Manufactured in the United States and printed on
acid-free paper. The paper used in this publication meets
the minimum requirements of ANSI/NISO Z39.48—1992
(R 1997) (*Permanence of Paper*).

FIRST AMERICAN EDITION

Design, composition, and illustrations by Katherine Messenger,
www.KatherineMessenger.com

LIBRARY OF CONGRESS CATALOGING-IN-PUBLICATION DATA

Names: Kirkpatrick, Melanie, author.
Title: Thanksgiving : the holiday at the heart of the American experience /
by Melanie Kirkpatrick.
Description: New York : Encounter Books, 2016. | Includes bibliographical
references and index.
Identifiers: LCCN 2016018851 (print) | LCCN 2016019723 (ebook) | ISBN 9781594038938
(hardcover : alk. paper) | ISBN 9781594038945 (Ebook)
Subjects: LCSH: Thanksgiving Day—History. | Holidays—United
States—History. | United States—Social life and customs.
Classification: LCC GT4975 .K54 2016 (print) | LCC GT4975 (ebook) | DDC
394.2649—dc23
LC record available at https://lccn.loc.gov/2016018851

To my sisters, Holly and Robin,
and the memory of our parents,
Bill and Virginia

CONTENTS

Newcomers

 few days before Thanksgiving, I took the subway from Manhattan to the New York City borough of Queens. It was one of those November mornings that signal Thanksgiving is near—a cloudless sky, temperatures bracing enough to warrant diving into the coat closet to locate a scarf and gloves, and the sight of fallen leaves swirling in a neighborhood garden as I walked to the subway station. When my train exited the tunnel under the East River and clattered aboveground into Queens, I could see the sun sparkling on the water down below. A couple of miles south of the bridge I had just crossed, the East River empties into New York Harbor. It mingles there with the Hudson River, which flows into the harbor from its parallel route along the west side of Manhattan.

When the one hundred and two English settlers now known as the Pilgrims sailed on the *Mayflower* in the autumn of 1620, they intended to land not far from this very spot. The ship's master, Christopher

Jones, was steering for the mouth of "Hudson's River." The Hudson, as the river would come to be called, formed the northernmost border of the Colony of Virginia, where the English Crown had given the Pilgrims permission to settle. But the turbulent seas and fierce winds of the Atlantic pushed the *Mayflower* off course. The ship overshot its destination, ending up off the tip of Cape Cod in what is now Massachusetts. It was November. Winter was coming. The *Mayflower* had been in transit for two months, and provisions were running dangerously low.

Master Jones informed the Pilgrim leaders that his ship could go no farther and told them to choose a spot to land. The Pilgrims selected a location with a deep harbor, an abundant source of fresh water, and a hill on which they could build a defensible fort. They named their new home Plymouth, after the English port city from which they had embarked on their journey to the New World. It became the first permanent European settlement in New England.

My destination in Queens that autumn morning was a public high school for recent immigrants. Newcomers High School was founded in 1995 for the purpose of providing new arrivals with intensive instruction in the English language and an introduction to American culture, along with the standard high school curriculum. Once they are proficient in English, the students have the option of transferring to a mainstream city high school. Newcomers is housed in an imposing four-story brick edifice in Long Island City. The building first opened its doors in 1905, when an earlier wave of immigrants arrived in New York City with children who needed to be educated.

Queens is one of the most ethnically diverse communities in America. It is home to 2.7 million New Yorkers, almost half of whom—47.7 percent, to be precise—were born in a foreign country, according to the 2010 U.S. Census. More than half of Queens residents speak a language other than English at home. The ethnic composition of students at Newcomers High reflects that diversity. On the day I visited, the school's eight hundred fifty students came from sixty-plus countries and spoke more than forty languages. If the Tower of Babel had a contemporary earthly home, it would be located in the corridors of Newcomers High.

For Newcomers' students, the coming holiday would be their first or second Thanksgiving. I was visiting the school at the invitation of two teachers who were teaching the history of the holiday even though it wasn't part of the state-mandated curriculum. A hundred years earlier, at the turn of the twentieth century, when immigrants were flooding into this country from many distant lands, school textbooks routinely included the history of Thanksgiving. Teaching newly arrived students about the history and traditions of the holiday was seen as a way to Americanize them, a way to help them establish ties to their new country. These days, while the basic history of Thanksgiving is still taught in elementary schools, it has mostly disappeared from high school curriculums. The teachers who invited me to speak to their classes in Queens were taking a cue from the past. They saw an opportunity to educate their foreign-born students about the early history of their new country as well as a way to help them understand a uniquely American holiday that is enjoyed by virtually every citizen.

I agreed to lead the class discussions because I wanted to hear what students had to say about the favorite holiday of their new country. What did these young people know about the origins of Thanksgiving? Were their families going to celebrate it? What did this uniquely American festival tell them—positive and negative—about the history, values, and culture of the United States?

Several years later, that day at Newcomers High is still vivid in my mind. As the school bell announced the start of my first class, eleventh-grade American history, I felt a little stab of nervousness. Sixteen-year-olds can be annoyingly taciturn. Would the kids slouching at the desks in front of me have anything to say about a holiday that many of them had never even celebrated? How would I encourage them to talk to me, especially those for whom English still didn't come easily? My sister Holly, a high school teacher, had advised me to avoid asking yes-no questions. Frame your questions in a manner that encourages the kids to speak expansively, she suggested. As it turned out, getting the students to speak up was not a problem. Anything but. The problem was keeping them from talking all at once. They had lots to say and were eager to talk. As our classroom conversation took shape, it did not take me long to realize that this group of teenagers, born in the four corners of the world, had much to teach a native-born visitor about the essential meaning of Thanksgiving.

These young newcomers had a very personal understanding of the earliest story at the heart of the American experience. For them, the Pilgrim story was *their* story, and the Pilgrim fathers and mothers were historical reflections of themselves. Some identified with the group of

Pilgrims known as Separatists, the religious dissenters who were seeking an opportunity to practice their faith freely. Others felt a kinship with the Strangers, the skilled workers and indentured servants who took passage on the *Mayflower* in the hope of building better lives for themselves and their families in the New World.

The teenagers understood the hurdles that the English settlers had to overcome before they celebrated the First Thanksgiving. More important, they understood why it was worth the risks. A boy from Bangladesh expressed it eloquently, if with imperfect grammar: "My story and their story was very much alike," he said. "Both groups suffered in their mother country...and arrived in the United States with a new hope in [their] heart, a new dream in [their] eyes."

For the students at Newcomers High, the Pilgrims' story mirrored their own experiences, and they exuberantly claimed the Thanksgiving holiday as their own. The Pilgrims "were looking for something they didn't have in England," explained a girl from Colombia. "When you come here it is the same. You have to face difficulties." An Ecuadorian girl sitting near her agreed: "When the Pilgrims came here, they felt alone and didn't have friends. Me either."

Other students shared similar personal tales: "My dad came here to have a better life," offered a girl from Ivory Coast. Her father had worked as a houseboy in his home country. Now he had a good job with the Metropolitan Transit Authority. Or a boy from China: "My mother finished elementary school. Then there wasn't any money for middle school.... She wanted to come here to make a better life for her children." Another Bangladeshi boy referred to the Declaration of Independence:

His family came here for the purpose of "pursuiting the happiness."

Like the Separatists—the Calvinist reformers who had rejected the Church of England—some of the students at Newcomers High came to the United States seeking freedom of worship. One boy told me he was from Tibet, a country that has not existed formally since China annexed it in 1950. He explained that his Buddhist family couldn't practice the religion of the Dalai Lama in China. A Christian student, born in the predominantly Muslim country of Indonesia, described how she was persecuted by Muslims in her neighborhood and feared for her safety. Another Christian, this one a Copt from Egypt, said she was afraid of being kidnapped and forced to convert to Islam. "We wanted to close all the bad pages of memory... and start a new page," she told me in describing her family's decision to move to the United States.

The students were so eager to talk that it was sometimes hard to keep up. The words flew across the room. Our conversation ranged far beyond the Pilgrims and the history of the First Thanksgiving. The students knew that a hallmark of the holiday was feasting, and soon the discussion segued to the poverty they observed in America, the land of plenty. They offered views on American generosity, on football, on the European settlers' displacement of the Native American peoples, on Abraham Lincoln's proclamation of Thanksgiving Day, and of course, on Thanksgiving dinner.

The kids were all familiar with Thanksgiving's food traditions and many said they planned to celebrate at home with the traditional meal. It would be the first time that some of them would taste turkey, a meat not widely available in many of their native countries. There would be nontraditional foods on the menu too, as their families initiated their own

Thanksgiving food traditions by incorporating favorite home-country dishes into the classic American meal. A Polish girl mentioned pierogies. A Chinese boy said his family would eat rice. When I asked whether it really matters what you eat on Thanksgiving, I got a bunch of you-gotta-be-kidding looks. "Yes! It's tradition!" one student shouted out. "Remember the history of the country," another student admonished. When it came to attitudes about Thanksgiving, the familiar metaphor of America as a melting pot certainly held true for this spirited group of teenagers.

The basic story of the First Thanksgiving is well known to every American: Pilgrims and Indians. Turkey and cranberries. Giving thanks. But few Americans know much more about the holiday's multifaceted history. Nor do we often stop to consider the role that Thanksgiving has played in many aspects of American life in the four centuries since the Pilgrims and the Wampanoag people feasted together for three days in what is now Plymouth, Massachusetts.

It was late summer or early autumn in 1621 when the Pilgrims who had survived their first winter in the New World sat down with their Wampanoag neighbors to share food and fellowship. The friendly coexistence between the English settlers and the Native Americans would last only a few decades longer. But that original Thanksgiving pointed the way to the diverse, multicultural people we have become.

In telling the history of Thanksgiving, I have taken my cue from the young immigrants I interviewed at Newcomers High School. Like my conversation with those enthusiastic newcomers, this book ranges widely, venturing into the realms of religion, hospitality, economics, philanthropy, culture, and politics, as well as food. It is not arranged chronologically. Rather, it weaves and bobs among the centuries to recount little-known stories about Thanksgiving that I hope will shed light on the meaning of America's favorite holiday and how it reflects and reinforces values most Americans share.

Thanksgiving is at the heart of the American experience. It is intertwined with seminal moments in our history—the arrival of the early European settlers, the Revolutionary War, the Civil War, the westward expansion, the influx of immigrants. In all these events, religious faith played a part. The first act of the first Continental Congress was to declare a national day of giving thanks to God. The first presidential proclamation was George Washington's call for a day of thanksgiving. In 1863, when the nation was torn asunder by war, Lincoln established the Thanksgiving holiday as a permanent fixture on the American calendar. Congress codified Thanksgiving Day into law in 1941, just days after the United States' entry into World War II.

In 1937, the historian Samuel Eliot Morison famously wrote that the Pilgrims are the "spiritual ancestors of all Americans whatever their stock, race or creed."[1] Today we live in more fractious times, often tending to focus more on what divides us than on what unites us. In my visit to Newcomers High School in Queens, I set out to discover whether Morison's sentiment holds true today in the minds of some of America's newest and youngest arrivals. Their answer was a resounding *yes*. So, too, say most Americans—at least on Thanksgiving Day.

CHAPTER ONE

The First Thanksgiving

It is a good thing to give thanks unto the Lord.
—Psalm 92

I am standing in the grand exhibition hall on the upper level of the Pilgrim Hall Museum in Plymouth, Massachusetts, admiring a painting titled *The First Thanksgiving at Plymouth*. The museum's amiable director, Patrick Browne, is about to give me a reality check.[1]

The First Thanksgiving at Plymouth is an iconic work of American art. It has appeared countless times in books, calendars, and greeting cards since it was created by Jennie Brownscombe in 1914. Most Americans would recognize it. Every American would know at a glance that its subject is Thanksgiving.

This is the First Thanksgiving as we picture it in our mind's eye. Pilgrims and Indians are gathered around a long dining table that is set outdoors on a beautiful autumn day. The sun is sparkling off flame-colored maple trees in the background; the placid waters of Plymouth Bay are visible in the distance. As I am silently taking in the painting, Patrick cuts into my thoughts. *The First Thanksgiving at Plymouth* is full of historical inaccuracies, he tells me. That is not what it looked like. The Pilgrims wore bright colors—reds, blues, greens, violets—not the sober hues pictured here. The Indians of New England never donned feathered headdresses, as in this painting, which seems to have been inspired by the Plains Indians of the American West. If there had been a table, the Pilgrim women would not have been seated with the men; they would have been busy preparing the food. The First Thanksgiving may not even have taken place in the fall; it could have been late summer, when the harvest would have been gathered. In short, there is not a whole lot that the artist seems to have gotten right about the event other than the fact that it was held outdoors. *The First Thanksgiving at Plymouth* is an interpretation, Patrick emphasizes, and we can enjoy it as such; but it is not historically accurate.

On that score—interpretation—it seems to me that Brownscombe's rendering of the First Thanksgiving deserves high marks. The focal point of the painting is an elderly Pilgrim who is saying grace. He is standing behind his seat at the table, head lifted to heaven, eyes closed, hands raised and clasped together in prayer. The artist may have fallen short on the historical details, but she captured the most important aspect of the First Thanksgiving and of every Thanksgiving that has followed: giving thanks.

Downstairs in another gallery are various artifacts that belonged to the Pilgrims. Many of them were brought over on the *Mayflower* and may have been used at that three-day harvest feast of 1621. These

ordinary household items hold at least as much power as Brownscombe's painting. View them, and the Pilgrims' story comes to life.

We start with Governor William Bradford's Bible. It is the 1560
Geneva translation, which the Pilgrims favored as more accurate than
the 1611 King James Version used by the Church of England. Most
Pilgrim households had a Geneva Bible, and the one on display was
printed in London in 1592. One of the Geneva Bible's most important innovations was to divide the text into verses as well as chapters.
Another was to use roman rather than gothic type. How much easier
these simple changes must have made it for ordinary readers to follow
and understand the words of the Bible.

Bradford's Bible embodies the entire history of the Pilgrims. This is
the volume that accompanied them through their voyages and whose
words sustained them through ordeal after ordeal. "You look at it and
you think of the fact that when the Pilgrim congregation was gathering together in England, William Bradford was reading this Bible,"
Patrick tells me. "When they went to Holland, he was reading this Bible. When they came over on the *Mayflower*, he was reading this Bible.
This is the Bible that was in that primitive little house he built a few
blocks over from here. And now it's right in front of us."

We move on to examine more Pilgrim belongings: Myles
Standish's sword; Peter Brown's beer tankard; Constance Hopkins's
beaver hat; and a pair of armless spectacles made of glass, horn, leather, and wood that belonged to an unknown Pilgrim, presumably
of middle age, whose eyesight was failing. There is a faded piece of
needlework made by Standish's daughter that is the earliest known

American-made sampler. It is long and narrow and embroidered with a pious verse that begins:

Loara Standish is my name

Lord guide my heart that I may do thy will.

We take a look at Myles Standish's iron cooking pot. It boasts two handles, convenient for lifting it on and off the hearth. In another display case is a large wooden bowl fashioned from burl maple. The bowl was used by the Wampanoag for preparing and serving food. It is one of the few Native American artifacts in the museum's collection.

We also see the cradle of the first European child to be born in New England. The cradle rocked Peregrine White, son of Susanna and William White. Susanna was pregnant when she and William and their five-year-old son Resolved boarded the *Mayflower*, and she knew she would need a safe place to lay a newborn infant.

Peregrine was born aboard the *Mayflower* as it lay at anchor off the tip of Cape Cod. It was late November 1620, a few weeks before a scouting team decided on Plymouth as the location for the Pilgrims' permanent settlement. Susanna and William chose a name for their son consistent with the circumstances of his birth. The name derives from the Latin word *peregrinus*, which means *wanderer* or *foreigner*, and is the source of the English word *pilgrim*. Like his fellow Pilgrims, little Peregrine was a stranger in a strange land. By the time of the First Thanksgiving in the late summer or early autumn of 1621, he would have been old enough to crawl.

Susanna White was one of eighteen Pilgrim wives who accompanied their husbands on the *Mayflower*. Several men left wives behind, planning to send for their families after they were established in America. Only four of the eighteen *Mayflower* wives survived to the time of the First Thanksgiving. Susanna lived, but her husband, William, died three months after Peregrine's birth, during the wretched first winter in Plymouth.

All together, only half of the men, women, and children who had sailed on the *Mayflower* were still alive a year after landing in the New World. Many fell victim to an illness that scholars theorize was a virulent form of influenza. The Pilgrims called it "the great sickness." Whatever it was, the weak, poorly nourished settlers started falling ill about two weeks after arriving in Plymouth. Most of the sick were crowded into the small common house that the settlers had managed to construct quickly. But not everyone could fit into it, so others were kept aboard the *Mayflower*, anchored in Plymouth Harbor. Both the ship and the common house were overcrowded, and the illness spread rapidly. The few people who stayed well had to prepare the food, get the water, and care for the sick.

As I examine the artifacts Patrick shows me, I wonder what role they might have played in the First Thanksgiving. Did Susanna set the cradle under the shade of a tree with baby Peregrine asleep inside, while she prepared food for the outdoor feasting? In *The First Thanksgiving at Plymouth*, Brownscombe paints Peregrine in his cradle, with Susanna seated nearby.

What of the cooking pot that belonged to Myles Standish and his late wife, Rose, who had died in January? Did the four surviving wives press the Standish cooking pot into service when they set about feeding the Pilgrims and their many Wampanoag guests? Constance Hopkins, then fourteen years old, surely lent a hand as the women worked. I can picture her wearing that wide-brimmed beaver hat with the peaked top. And what of Governor Bradford himself? Did he read aloud from his Bible to the assembled Pilgrims? Did he take a break from the hubbub and seek a quiet corner to read the Scriptures by himself?

Many of the Pilgrim artifacts have sorrowful stories associated with them—the cradle that rocked a fatherless child, the cooking pot that often would have been empty for lack of food to put in it, the sword whose owner was prepared to use it against the "savages" he expected to encounter. In the face of such sadness, deprivation, and terror, how is it that in the late summer or early autumn of 1621, the Pilgrims came together with grateful hearts to celebrate their first harvest in the New World and give thanks?

There are two eyewitness accounts of the First Thanksgiving. William Bradford, Plymouth's longtime governor, penned one.[2] Edward Winslow is the author of the other. Both accounts are brief but vivid. Bradford's weighs in at one hundred sixty-seven words. Winslow's is only one hundred fifty-one words.[3] Read them and you find yourself in familiar territory. As described by the two Pilgrim leaders, the event that Americans have come to call the First Thanksgiving was remarkably similar to the holiday we mark today. There was feasting and game playing, and an all-round mood of good cheer.

In their separate accounts, Bradford and Winslow each make much of the bounty on hand in New England, an abundance that presages the dining tables at modern-day Thanksgiving dinners. Bradford tells of the "great store of wild turkeys, of which they took many." He also notes the "cod and bass and other fish, of which they took good store." Winslow offers an anecdote about the rich natural resources of the American continent that would have wowed his readers back in England. The governor dispatched a shooting party for the occasion, he writes, and the four Pilgrims killed enough birds in one day to serve the community for almost a week.

It is from Winslow that we learn that a large group of Wampanoag warriors joined the Pilgrim feast. In telling how the Pilgrims welcomed the Wampanoag to their celebration, Winslow homes in on other attributes of the holiday, then and now: hospitality, generosity, neighborliness. He describes, too, how the guests returned the favor. The Wampanoags' "greatest king Massasoit" and his men "went out and killed five deer," which they "bestowed on our Governor [Bradford], and upon the Captain [Myles Standish] and others." So, too, a modern guest, upon accepting an invitation to Thanksgiving dinner, is likely to ask his host: What can I bring?

The central similarity between the First Thanksgiving and today's holiday is something less tangible: the spirit of thankfulness. From the first, as Bradford and Winslow imply, Thanksgiving has been a time to stop and take stock of the blessings enjoyed by family and community. As the English settlers overcame the trials they faced that first year in Plymouth, qualities that Americans have come to honor as integral to our national identity were on full display: courage, perseverance, diligence, piety. These are the virtues that helped to shape the American character.

The Pilgrims displayed another virtue, one they practiced every day and which stood at the heart of the First Thanksgiving. Cicero called it the greatest of the virtues and the parent of all the rest: gratitude.

And yet, here is an odd thing—odd, at least, for the modern-day reader of the Pilgrims' accounts. The word "thanksgiving" does not appear in either description. Neither Bradford nor Winslow referred to the feast as Thanksgiving.

If you could travel back in time to 1621, tap a Pilgrim on the shoulder, and ask him to define "Thanksgiving Day," his answer might surprise you. For the Pilgrims, a "day of thanksgiving" was not marked by feasting, family, and fellowship—the happy hallmarks of the holiday we now celebrate. It was a different matter altogether.

The Pilgrims brought with them from England a religious custom of marking days of thanksgiving, along with their counterpart, days of fasting and humiliation. Days of thanksgiving, usually including a communal meal, were called in response to specific beneficences such as a successful harvest, propitious weather, or a military victory.[4] Fast days were called to pray for God's help and guidance in time of trouble or difficulty. For the Pilgrims, then, a "thanksgiving day" was imbued with religious meaning, and set aside for prayer and worship.

Some contemporary observers like to stress this historical usage, arguing that the event known today as the First Thanksgiving was therefore not a true "thanksgiving day." These naysayers aren't just being Thanksgiving Scrooges. They are right that the Pilgrims would not have viewed the harvest feast of 1621 as a thanksgiving in their understanding of the word. But it is also true that the spirit of gratitude was very much present on that occasion. The Pilgrims may not have called it a thanksgiving, but there is no reason we shouldn't do so.

William DeLoss Love, a nineteenth-century scholar of the religious days of thanksgiving in New England, eloquently expressed this point of view when, in 1895, he wrote about the First Thanksgiving: "It was not a thanksgiving at all, judged by their Puritan customs, which they kept in 1621; but as we look back upon it after nearly three centuries, it seems so wonderfully like the day we love that we claim it as the progenitor of our harvest feasts."[5]

The day we love, to use Love's affectionate words, owes a debt to both of these traditions—the harvest feast of 1621 and the New England colonies' religious days of thanksgiving.

The Pilgrims were world-class practitioners of the virtue of gratitude. They gave thanks in their morning prayers and again in the grace they said before and after every meal, and once more in their evening devotions. As they went about their work, the Pilgrims would sing psalms, hymns of praise and thanksgiving. The congregation sang psalms, too, in their Sunday worship services. The music and text they followed came from the Ainsworth Psalter, a book of psalms published in Holland in 1612 and one of the volumes they brought with them on the *Mayflower*. In some sense, the Pilgrims viewed every day as a thanksgiving day, certainly including the days of the 1621 feast that has come to be known as the First Thanksgiving.

There is no written record of prayers spoken by the Pilgrims on that occasion, or any other day. This is not surprising. The Pilgrims did not believe in reciting set prayers, which they viewed as forced and inauthentic, and they rejected the Church of England's magisterial Book of Common Prayer, which contains some of the most beautiful poetry in the English language. John Robinson, the Pilgrims' pastor when they resided in England and Holland, warned of "counterfeit" prayers. He wrote: "We may say prayers, and sing prayers and read prayers, and hear prayers, and yet not pray."[6] Set prayers were considered a barrier between the individual and God. Rather, the Pilgrims practiced extemporaneous, individual prayer. Each person was responsible for communicating directly with the Almighty, using the words of his choice.

As we learn from Bradford's journal, Winslow's letter, and other documents of the day, the Pilgrims had numerous reasons to give thanks that autumn.

The most important was the chance to practice their religion freely. This was the reason they had uprooted themselves from their refuge in Holland and risked everything to settle in the wilderness of North America.

The Pilgrims were Puritans, or English Protestant reformers who followed the teachings of John Calvin. The name "Puritan" derived from their aim to "purify" the Church of England, which they believed clung too closely to its Roman Catholic roots. While some Puritans were willing to work for reform within the Church of England, others took a more radical view. They broke away and established their own tiny congregation in the village of Scrooby, in Nottinghamshire, thus coming to be called Separatists. When the Crown tried to have them arrested and jailed for refusing to take part in Church of England rituals, the congregation fled in 1608 to Holland, which permitted the free practice of religion. The Separatists spent more than a decade in the Dutch city of Leiden. They were allowed to worship freely, but they struggled to make a living and they worried that their children were growing up more Dutch than English. So they pulled up stakes again and crossed the ocean to the New World.

At the time of the First Thanksgiving, the Pilgrims had a second reason to rejoice: their survival. They gave thanks for having made it through the previous winter, when cold, famine, and disease killed half of their original number. The fifty-three surviving Pilgrims included twenty-two men, four women, five teenage girls, nine teenage boys, and thirteen small children and infants.[7]

Peace with their Wampanoag neighbors was a third reason for the Pilgrims to give thanks. Their friendship with the Wampanoag people was a welcome and unexpected development. They had negotiated a peace treaty with Massasoit, the sachem, or chief, of the tribal confederation of Indians who inhabited coastal Massachusetts and Rhode Island. When Massasoit and his men showed up at the First Thanksgiving, the Pilgrims welcomed them and entertained them for three days.

In sheer numbers, Massasoit and his men overwhelmed the Pilgrims at the celebration. In his letter to his unnamed friend in London, Winslow is specific about the number of Indians who joined them for their feast. Massasoit brought with him ninety men, he writes. That number—nearly double the size of the Pilgrim band—speaks volumes about the peaceful ties between the two peoples. If they had been so minded, the Wampanoag warriors might have overpowered the English easily enough. The Pilgrims had the advantage of possessing guns, but they had not had time to build a fort or other defenses, and the number of fighting-age men was a mere twenty-two. The settlers had taken pains earlier that year, during the time of the great sickness, to ensure that their Indian neighbors did not find out how low their numbers had dwindled, burying their dead at night. Now they were taking the risk of exposing their entire community in full view of Massasoit and his men.

The Pilgrims were on their guard—Winslow records that they "exercised their arms," presumably in a display of power as well as for entertainment. But they sat down together with the Wampanoag as friends, and the friendship would endure for fifty years.

The Pilgrim leaders recognized the debt they owed the Wampanoag tribal confederation—which was a fourth reason to give thanks. Without the practical assistance of the Wampanoag, the Pilgrims' first harvest in the New World almost certainly would have failed. Tisquantum, the Patuxet Indian whom the English dubbed Squanto, was indispensable. He taught them how to plant corn using fish as fertilizer, and he directed them to the best hunting grounds and fishing spots. Bradford praised Squanto as "a special instrument sent of God."[8]

It was two years later, in 1623, that the Pilgrims held their first official "day of thanksgiving" as they understood the concept. The occasion was a rainfall that saved their harvest and their lives. If the harvest had failed, famine was sure to follow and the settlement of Plymouth might not have survived.

A drought began in the third week of May, just after planting—the worst possible timing. The Pilgrims' winter food stores were depleted and their diet depended heavily on their luck at fishing. "God fed them out of the sea for the most part," Bradford writes. A lobster, some fish, a drink of spring water—that was a typical meal. In the middle of July, as the corn began to shrivel and the ground was "parched like withered hay," Bradford ordered a day of fasting "to seek the Lord by humble and fervent prayer."

The day of the fast dawned hot, with clear, cloudless skies. There was no sign of rain. Then, toward evening, clouds formed, the sky grew overcast, and it began to rain. The rain fell "with such sweet and gentle showers as gave them cause of rejoicing and blessing God," Bradford records. The rain then started to fall heavily, in such abundance "that the earth was thoroughly wet and soaked." The corn and other crops revived. It was "wonderful to see," and the Indians were "astonished." Bradford promptly called a day of thanksgiving.[9]

All the New England colonies followed the custom of designating days of public thanksgiving in response to specific events. The first of these designated days in the Massachusetts Bay Colony occurred in July 1630 after the colonists' safe arrival. The second took place in February 1631, when a ship from England that had been believed to be lost at sea arrived in Boston Harbor bringing badly needed supplies for the hungry colonists.

The early Dutch settlers in what is today New York City also marked days of thanksgiving. One of the earliest recorded in New Netherland occurred in 1644, after Dutch troops launched a moonlight raid on an Indian village near Stamford, Connecticut. The bloody Dutch-Indian skirmishes continued over the next year, until the warring sides finally concluded a peace treaty. That prompted another call for a day of thanksgiving, on the sixth of September 1645. This proclamation specified that church services be held in the morning so that "God Almighty may be specially thanked, praised, and blessed."[10]

Dutch days of thanksgiving were less solemn than New England ones. In New Amsterdam, a more mercantile environment than agricultural New England, work and amusements usually were forbidden only during the hours of the church services, not all day long. When afternoon or evening arrived, the Dutch were free to feast, play games, and enjoy military displays.[11]

In 1654, the Dutch issued a proclamation for a day of thanksgiving to celebrate a peace treaty between England and the Netherlands. The proclamation ordered citizens to attend worship services in the morning and then went on to tell them to enjoy themselves in the evening: "After the public worship shall be performed," citizens were called upon "to indulge in all moderate festivities and rejoicings as the event recommends and their situation shall permit."[12]

At some point in the 1600s, the New England colonies began to designate annual thanksgiving days, usually in the autumn, around the time of the harvest. These celebrations were deemed "general" thanksgivings—not for a specific event or blessing, but for continuing blessings. They were usually called by civil rather than religious authorities. These were steps toward the holiday we know today.

Connecticut was the first to make Thanksgiving an annual event. In 1639, the colony proclaimed the first in a series of thanksgivings for ordinary blessings. According to the Public Records of the Colony of Connecticut, on August 26, 1639, the General Court of Connecticut "concluded that there be a public day of thanksgiving in these plantations upon the 18th of next month."[13]

The custom of a thanksgiving for general blessings did not catch on in Massachusetts until later in the seventeenth century, and then only after a spirited theological debate. The losing side argued that an annual thanksgiving for general reasons would make people take God's generosity for granted. In the words of one opponent, an annual thanksgiving would "tend to harden the people in their carnal confidence."[14]

Under New England law, days of thanksgiving were treated like the Sabbath—as days of rest. Work and entertainments were banned. Violators faced fines and other punishments.

In 1696, an unlucky man by the name of William Veazie, a church warden in Houghs Neck, Massachusetts—now part of the city of Quincy, near Boston—was charged with failing to properly observe a day of public thanksgiving. According to court records, on the morning of that day, Veazie was seen at his farm plowing a field of corn "with an Indian Boy and Two Horses." He pleaded guilty and was fined ten pounds.

That wasn't all. The court further sentenced Veazie to "be set in the pillory in the market place in Boston to morrow about noon, there to stand by the Space of An Hour." Pillorying an offender in the heart of the city at the busiest time of day sent a potent message to all who passed: Respect Thanksgiving Day.[15]

Statutes regulating Thanksgiving Day behavior were still in force in New England in the nineteenth century, though the pillory's days were past. In 1825, a Connecticut man named Gladwin contested the service of a civil process on Thanksgiving Day. He argued that the constable's delivery of the writ was invalid since there was a law against working on Thanksgiving. The state supreme court agreed.

In support of its ruling, the court cited the state statute pertaining to days of thanksgiving: "All persons shall abstain from every kind of servile labour and vain recreation, works of necessity and mercy excepted." The service of a civil process, the court ruled, was neither a work of necessity nor an act of mercy. Gladwin won his case.[16]

It is impossible to know precisely when the feasting and family aspects of Thanksgiving Day began to overtake the religious ones, but the trend appears to have started toward the end of the seventeenth century. That is when Thanksgiving dinner grew in importance in New England, "adding homecoming relatives, extra pies and platters of roast meat," in the words of the historian Diana Karter Appelbaum. Churches accommodated the custom of a festive dinner by eliminating the afternoon service on Thanksgiving Day, "first in the country districts where the walk to meeting was long and cold," Appelbaum writes, "then in 1720 in Boston itself." Soon Thanksgiving dinner was nearly as important as the morning prayer service.[17]

Thanksgiving wouldn't be Thanksgiving without someone lamenting this trend and calling on Americans to focus their attention less on feasting and more on giving thanks. In 1792, the *Connecticut Courant* published a letter from a man complaining that Thanksgiving had become a day devoted to eating and drinking.[18] In 1873, an article published in the *Boston Daily Globe* on the day after Thanksgiving bemoaned the decline in the religious character of the day:

"The views of our Puritan ancestors in regard to attendance on divine worship were disregarded...but the revered turkey was trotted out with all the alacrity which good housewives are wont to expect."[19] In 1926, an editorial in an educational journal complained that "The religious significance of the day touches many not at all, the historical significance is quite forgotten.... Are we so self-sufficient that gratitude and acknowledgement are inappropriate?"[20]

Still, the religious aspects of the holiday continue to touch many Americans today. Chances are good that before you begin your Thanksgiving dinner, you pause for a moment or more to give thanks. For many Americans, perhaps most, giving thanks means saying a prayer. On an ordinary day, 44 percent of Americans say grace before eating, according to one survey. Another 44 percent of Americans report they almost never say grace—a response that implies they do so on special occasions such as Thanksgiving Day.[21] Almost every religion practiced in the United States encourages the celebration of Thanksgiving. One exception is Jehovah's Witnesses, who do not celebrate any holiday that is not based on the Bible.

Americans are a religious people—a strong majority profess a belief in God—and on Thanksgiving Day, they usually express their gratitude to the Almighty in whatever form that being takes shape in their faith. While the custom of attending religious services on Thanksgiving Day has long since lapsed, and the holiday is not tied to any particular religion, for many Americans the opening words of the old Thanksgiving hymn still apply: "We gather together to ask the Lord's blessings."

Nonreligious Americans find secular ways to express gratitude. Some families go around the Thanksgiving table asking each person, young and old, to name something for which he or she is grateful. Others pause to express gratitude to the cooks who made the meal, the farmers who grew the food, the love of family and friends, the blessings of liberty, or simply for their general good fortune. For the late author Ayn Rand, an atheist, the essential meaning of Thanksgiving was "a celebration of successful production." The lavish meal, she wrote, is "a symbol of the fact that abundant consumption is the result and reward of production. Abundance is (or was and ought to be) America's pride—just as it is the pride of American parents that their children need never know starvation."[22]

In his lovely little book *The Thanksgiving Ceremony*, published in 2003, Edward Bleier, a Jew and the son of immigrants from Eastern Europe, describes a ritual he composed for use around the Thanksgiving table.[23] Bleier's twenty-minute ceremony acknowledges God but is nonsectarian. The ceremony is inspired by the Passover Seder, which celebrates the Jews' liberation from slavery in Egypt as told in the biblical book of Exodus. *The Thanksgiving Ceremony* recounts the Pilgrim story, and includes brief readings from the Declaration of Independence, Lincoln's Thanksgiving Proclamation, a speech by Martin Luther King, and other notable American texts. It concludes with the singing of "America the Beautiful."

Bleier's Thanksgiving ceremony reflects another aspect of Thanksgiving Day gratitude that has become part of the holiday: love of country. Since the Revolution, Thanksgiving has become a patriotic holiday, a time to give thanks for the blessings of liberty as enshrined in the American system of government. Presidential Thanksgiving Proclamations end with the date expressed in both the ordinary way and as "year X of the Independence of the United States."

Nearly four hundred years after the First Thanksgiving, gratitude is still the byword of the day. On the fourth Thursday of November, most Americans, believers and nonbelievers, take seriously the custom of pausing to give thanks. This is the essential meaning of the Thanksgiving holiday. It was also the meaning of the days of thanksgiving marked by the Europeans who preceded the Pilgrims on this continent.

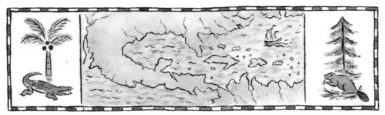

CHAPTER TWO

Before the Pilgrims

Although we are grateful to the English pilgrims who endured hardships and faced formidable risks to help colonize America, the Thanksgiving decreed by the Spaniard Don Juan de Oñate deserves equal credit and its own place in American history. — Ann W. Richards, Governor of Texas, 1991

A few weeks before Thanksgiving Day 1991, anyone who happened to be strolling along Court Street in downtown Plymouth would have witnessed a curious sight: a group of unfamiliar men dressed in doublets, wearing odd-shaped metal helmets festooned with feathers, and brandishing swords. What brought a company of sixteenth-century Spanish *conquistadores* to the heart of this classic New England town, home of the Pilgrim Mothers and Fathers?

All became clear when one of the *conquistadores* opened his mouth and, in a smooth Texas drawl, started speaking heresy: Plymouth did not deserve to be called the home of the First Thanksgiving, he announced. The true First Thanksgiving in what became the United States of America, he said, took place in San Elizario, Texas, a town twenty miles south of El Paso along the Rio Grande. In April

1598, Spanish settlers and Native Americans broke bread together in a feast that deserves to be acknowledged as America's First Thanksgiving.

Plymouth's response? The *conquistadores* were duly "arrested," jailed, and charged with "spreading malicious and false rumors and blasphemy." After a mock trial, they were acquitted on the basis of insufficient evidence and released.

This little drama on the streets of Plymouth was, of course, a show—a good-natured publicity stunt orchestrated by Texan history buffs eager to draw attention to their hometown of San Elizario and the role it played in the early history of the United States. The next year, Plymouth returned the favor, dispatching a contingent of local selectmen dressed as Pilgrims to Texas. They, too, were "arrested," "tried," and "convicted," then pardoned at the base of the gallows.[1]

This was all good fun—not to mention excellent PR for both towns. As a matter of historical record, however, the Texans had a point. History shows that the Pilgrims weren't the first Europeans to hold religious services of thanksgiving in the New World, nor were they the first European settlers to sit together with Native Americans at a thanksgiving table in the land that became the United States.

Most of the pre-Pilgrim thanksgivings were celebrated by European newcomers in parts of the country far from New England. More often than not, these were religious ceremonies called for the purpose of giving thanks for the Europeans' safe arrival in North America. The Age of Exploration was also an age of prayer, and the safe conclusion of a dangerous journey was just one of many reasons for a Christian to kneel and give thanks.

The pre-Plymouth thanksgivings were mostly religious observances—Protestant prayer services or Catholic Masses. A couple of them included a festive component, in the form of a meal and perhaps some entertainment. At least one thanksgiving—at Popham Colony in present-day Maine in 1607—was in part a harvest festival.

Several of the early thanksgivings celebrated by Europeans in the New World were shared with Native Americans, who observed the religious ceremonies, contributed food to a meal, or assisted the Europeans in other ways. None apparently took the large role that the Wampanoag played in Plymouth in helping the English to thrive. As in Plymouth, relations between the Europeans and indigenous people would degenerate in the years that followed, but for a moment in time, ties between the two peoples were harmonious, if wary.

The motivation of the modern-day claimants to the title of First Thanksgiving is easy to explain as local pride coupled with an eagerness to highlight local history. But it is also true that success has many friends. San Elizario and other locations with events in their early history that might be deemed Thanksgivings hoped to ride on the coattails of the New England Thanksgiving that Americans know and love. It is easy to smile when a town publicizes itself as a competitor to Plymouth, but there is a serious aspect to such claims. They are reminders that all the newcomers to our shores felt grateful to be here and found ways to express their gratitude.

There are at least seven claimants for the title of "First Thanksgiving"—in Texas, Virginia, Florida, and Maine. The Big Three are

San Elizario, Texas (1598); St. Augustine, Florida (1565); and Berkeley Plantation, Virginia (1619).

San Elizario, Texas. On April 30, 1598, an expedition traveling north from Mexico held a Roman Catholic service of thanksgiving along the banks of the Rio Grande. Led by the Spanish explorer Don Juan de Oñate y Salazar, the travelers had set up camp at what is now the dusty town of San Elizario.

Oñate, the son of a Spanish noble family, had been commissioned by King Philip II to seize the land north of the Rio Grande and claim it for the Spanish Empire. His expeditionary force included more than four hundred men, women, and children. Some were soldiers ready to fight to secure the Spanish claims; others were settlers prepared to take up residence in the uncharted territories of Nueva México. The settlers brought with them thousands of sheep, pigs, goats, cattle, mules, and horses for use in their new homes, and the expedition stretched for miles as it wended its way north from Santa Barbara in central Mexico toward the Rio Grande. By the time the travelers reached what is now San Elizario, they had been on the road for three months and had traveled hundreds of miles across the unforgiving terrain of the Chihuahuan Desert.

The expedition's scribe, Captain Gaspar Pérez de Villagrá, chronicled the journey in an epic poem, *Historica de la Nueva México.* Villagrá provides vivid descriptions of the San Elizario Thanksgiving and the circumstances leading up to it.[2]

By the time the expedition reached the Rio Grande, Villagrá writes, the travelers had been without food or water for four days. Their suffering was so intense that they "were almost all wishing for death."[3] Horses staggered into the river, drinking so much that two of the animals died when their full stomachs burst. Two additional horses, blinded by starvation, ventured too far into the rushing water and were swept away. The two-legged travelers also drank their fill. Thirsty men drank so much that they appeared to be drunk. In Villagrá's evocative words, they were:

> *Stretched out upon the watery sand,*
> *As swollen, dropsical, gasping,*
> *As they had all been toads...* [4]

Having assuaged their thirst, the toad-travelers rested under the cottonwood trees along the river for ten days, gathering strength and preparing to move on.

But before they resumed their journey, Oñate called for a day of thanksgiving, ordering that a makeshift church be created in a clearing in the woods. He commanded that the clearing for the thanksgiving Mass be large enough to hold the entire expeditionary force and an unspecified number of Indians.

When the appointed day arrived, Franciscan missionaries who were traveling with the expedition sang Mass, and Oñate read a proclamation known as *La Toma*—the Taking—declaring that he was claiming all the land north of the Rio Grande for Spain. Then a play—a "great drama," writes Villagrá—was performed for the benefit of the Indians, depicting how all of New Mexico welcomed the arrival of the Catholic Church. It was the first play performed in what is now the United States.

Villagrá characterizes the Spaniards' relations with the Indians as peaceful and friendly. The "great numbers of barbarian warriors" were helpful to the Spanish, and the Spanish were respectful and kind to the warriors, "showing ourselves agreeable friends."[5] The Indians directed the Spanish to a safe place for the expedition to cross the river: "the "passage," or *el paso*, which gave its name to the city that grew up there. The poet also describes in colorful detail a feast that took place while Oñate's expedition was resting at San Elizario—though possibly not on the day of thanksgiving itself. The Spanish shot cranes, ducks, and geese for the meal, and the Indians contributed fish. The meat and fish were cooked on spits and in the coals of a great bonfire. The day after their thanksgiving ceremony, the Spaniards packed up and moved on.

Historica de la Nueva México was published in 1610, but it took almost four centuries for the San Elizario Thanksgiving to become well known. In the late 1980s, local history buffs in San Elizario took up the story and used it to promote their town as a tourist destination. They inaugurated a festival that included re-enactments of La Toma and the Thanksgiving feast; they initiated a friendly competition with Plymouth about which town deserved to call itself the home of the First Thanksgiving; and they drummed up local media coverage, which in turn generated attention in the national press.

State politicians also took up the cause. In 1990, the Texas House of Representatives passed a resolution proclaiming that the First Thanksgiving in the United States had been held at San Elizario, not

Plymouth. In 1991, Governor Ann Richards issued a proclamation declaring April 28, 1598 as "the first true Thanksgiving in the United States,"[6] and, in what must go down in history as one of the biggest acts of Texas chutzpah, she called upon the governor of Massachusetts to follow suit. In 1995, Governor George W. Bush appointed a commission to plan activities to mark the quadricentennial in 1998 of Oñate's colonizing mission. In 2001, Governor Rick Perry proclaimed April 30 as the official day of the First Thanksgiving for Texas.

In recent years, Texans have backed off a bit on the idea of San Elizario as the home of the true First Thanksgiving. San Elizarians still host a Thanksgiving festival at the end of April, with a re-enactment of the 1598 ceremony, but the proceedings focus broadly on the early history of the region. A recent festival included a scholarly discussion of the role of Franciscan missionaries, a history of viticulture in the Southwest, and a presentation on seventeenth-century musical instruments.

Al Borrego, president of the local Genealogical and Historical Society, sums up Texans' new attitude on the First Thanksgiving when he asks: "Are we going to get the president of the United States to change the date of Thanksgiving?" Borrego answers his own question: "I don't think so." Besides, he adds, "I like turkey."[7]

St. Augustine, Florida. Some years before the San Elizario *conquistadores* were parading down the streets of Plymouth to promote their 1598 First Thanksgiving, a historian was laboring quietly at his desk at the

University of Florida in Gainesville researching earlier thanksgiving celebrations that occurred near present-day St. Augustine. Michael V. Gannon, a scholar of Florida's colonial history, quotes Juan Ponce de León in the opening pages of his book *The Cross in the Sand*:

"Thanks be to Thee, O Lord, Who has permitted me to see something new," said the Spanish explorer upon sighting the shore of the lush tropical land he would name *La Florida*. The year was 1513.[8] Ponce de León may have been the first European to speak words of thanksgiving in what is now the United States.

Half a century after Ponce de León had "discovered" it, another Spanish fleet set sail for Florida, this time under the command of Captain-General Pedro Menéndez de Avilés. General Menéndez had two mandates from King Philip II. One was missionary, the other military: convert the Indians to Christianity, and secure Florida for Spain. The king was worried about a settlement by French Huguenots in Florida during the previous year. He saw the French settlement as a direct challenge to Spain's rightful sovereignty over the peninsula and their Protestant religion as a threat to Roman Catholicism.

Menéndez's fleet reached the coast of Florida in early September 1565, carrying eight hundred colonists. On September 6, he sailed into the harbor at the place he would name St. Augustine, anchoring just off the Timucua Indian village of Seloy. The fleet chaplain, Father Francisco López de Mendoza Grajales, kept notes of the voyage and described the sequence of events leading up to the day of thanksgiving called to express thanks to God for the Spaniards' safe arrival.

An advance party made up of two companies of infantrymen disembarked and were "well-received by the Indians," Father López wrote. The Timucua gave the Spanish a large house that belonged to a chief and was well situated alongside the river. Worried that the Indians' friendliness might not hold, the Spanish went to work fortifying the house and building a trench around it to protect themselves from surprise attack. Two days later, on Saturday, September 8, General Menéndez was ready to come ashore.

The general's landing was full of pomp and circumstance. The priest recorded how Menéndez stepped onto Florida soil "with many banners spread" and "to the sound of trumpets and salutes of artillery." Father López, who had gone ashore the evening before, went to meet the general, carrying a cross and singing *Te Deum Laudamus*, or "Thee, O God, We Praise," a Latin hymn traditionally sung on occasions of public rejoicing. A makeshift altar was set up in the sand. "The General, followed by all who accompanied him, marched up to the Cross, knelt, and kissed it," Father López recounted. As a large number of Timucua watched, the newcomers celebrated a thanksgiving Mass. Afterward, the Timucua joined the Spanish for a meal at the invitation of General Menéndez. Professor Gannon describes the event as "the first community act of religion and thanksgiving in the first permanent settlement in the land."[9]

Historians who have analyzed the ship's accounts say the menu was probably the Spaniards' usual shipboard fare: salted pork, onions, garbanzo beans—possibly assembled in a bean stew called *cocido* and washed down with red wine. There is no record of what, if anything, the Timucua contributed, though some have conjectured that they would have offered something for the communal meal—maybe local game, possibly including wild turkey, which was plentiful at the time. The Timucua might also have brought seafood, maize, beans, nuts, and fruit.

Two decades passed before Gannon's research on the St. Augustine Thanksgiving became widely known. In the mid-1980s, an Associated Press reporter, seeking a new angle for an article he was writing on the holiday, stumbled upon Gannon's work, called him up, and then wrote about what happened in 1565. The AP story was picked up by the national media, and soon Gannon found himself with a new nickname, courtesy of New Englanders who were disgruntled that the Sunshine State was encroaching on their holiday. The Florida professor was now "the Grinch Who Stole Thanksgiving."

Berkeley Plantation, Virginia. The Commonwealth of Virginia's claim to hosting the First Thanksgiving rests on an event that happened on December 4, 1619. On that day, the English ship *Margaret* dropped anchor in the James River at what was then known as Berkeley Hundred and is now called Berkeley Plantation. It is located twenty-four miles southwest of Richmond.

The *Margaret* was carrying thirty-six Englishmen—farmers, craftsmen, and other skilled workers—who were committed to building a successful settlement in the New World. They had departed England ten weeks earlier under a commission from the London-based Berkeley Company to settle eight thousand acres of land along the James

River. These settlers hoped to avoid the fate of Jamestown, which had failed in part because the cavaliers and courtiers who went there in 1607 knew little about farming or other skills essential to the colony's survival. The *Margaret* party's captain, John Woodlief, was an experienced settler, one of the few survivors of the 1609–1610 starving time in Jamestown, when 80 percent of the colonists died.

After the new settlers rowed ashore, Captain Woodlief commanded them to kneel, and he led them in a prayer of thanksgiving for their safe arrival. This was done in accordance with the charter that had been issued by their sponsors in England. The instruction to hold such a service upon their arrival in Virginia was the first of ten orders listed in a letter that the Berkeley Company had handed to Captain Woodlief prior to the settlers' departure from England. In addition to the instruction that the settlers give thanks on the day of their arrival, the letter further ordered them to make the date of their arrival an annual day of thanksgiving:

> We ordain that the day of our ship's arrival at the place assigned for plantation in the land of Virginia should be yearly and perpetually kept holy as a day of Thanksgiving to Almighty God.[10]

The Berkeley Hundred Thanksgiving was a strictly religious affair, in keeping with other instructions the settlers received from their sponsor: Follow the rites of the Church of England, use the Book of Common Prayer, and attend daily prayers or forfeit supper. No Native Americans were present at the service, and there is no record of the settlers partaking in a festive meal.

As Virginians like to point out, the Berkeley Hundred Thanksgiving service in 1619 was the first "official" Thanksgiving in the sense that December 4 became the date of an annual observance. The settlers carried on the tradition for two more years, but Berkeley Hundred was destroyed on March 22, 1622, in a coordinated attack by the Powhatan Indians on English settlements in Virginia. Many settlers died in the attack, including a large number at Berkeley Hundred. Soon afterward, the settlement was abandoned and the survivors returned to England.

The story of Virginia's First Thanksgiving was lost to history for more than three hundred years. It was finally rediscovered in 1931 when Dr. Lyon Tyler, a retired president of William and Mary College and son of President John Tyler, was researching a book on early Virginia history at the New York Public Library. There he happened upon the Nibley Papers, a cache of documents that chronicled the *Margaret*'s voyage to Virginia and recorded the establishment, settlement, and management of the Berkeley Hundred. The Nibley Papers included the original instructions to Captain Woodlief to mark an annual day of thanksgiving. That "one little fact" made the rediscovery of the Nibley Papers "conspicuous in American history," Tyler concluded. It proved, he crowed, that the Virginia Thanksgiving of 1619 anticipated the one in Plymouth by two years.[11]

Dr. Tyler's discovery of the Nibley Papers sparked a campaign to revive the Virginia Thanksgiving, which had last been celebrated in 1621. A Virginia state senator, John J. Wicker Jr., took up the cause in the late 1950s. He traveled to Boston, where he met with the governor of Massachusetts in an effort to persuade him that Virginia was the site of the true First Thanksgiving. (No luck on that score—no surprise.) Wicker's enthusiasm for his cause drove him to don the garb of a seventeenth-century English settler and go on *The Tonight Show Starring Johnny Carson* to plead the case for Virginia to replace Plymouth as the home of the First Thanksgiving. In 1958, three hundred thirty-seven years after the third annual Thanksgiving Day at Berkeley Plantation, Virginians revived the tradition begun by the original settlers there and held a "Virginia Thanksgiving Festival." (The Virginia Thanksgiving Festival is now an annual event, celebrated on the first Sunday of November.)

Four years later, in November 1962, President John F. Kennedy issued a Thanksgiving proclamation that, to most readers, would have sounded completely routine. It began:

> Over three centuries ago in Plymouth, on Massachusetts Bay, the Pilgrims established the custom of gathering together each year to express their gratitude to God for the preservation of their community and for the harvests their labors brought forth in the new land. Joining with their neighbors, they shared together and worshipped together in a common giving of thanks.

Plymouth, Pilgrims, harvests, gratitude to God—all in keeping with the long string of presidential Thanksgiving proclamations. It contained nothing out of the ordinary. But John Wicker saw something wrong.

The Virginia state senator immediately shot off a telegram to

Kennedy. "Your Presidential Proclamation erroneously credits Massachusetts Pilgrims with America's First Thanksgiving observances," he complained. "America's First Thanksgiving was actually celebrated in Virginia in 1619, more than a year before the Pilgrims ever landed and nearly two years before the Massachusetts Thanksgiving." He concluded: "Please issue an appropriate correction."

Wicker received his reply three weeks later in the form of an apologetic letter from Arthur Schlesinger Jr., the eminent historian who was then a special assistant to the president. "You are quite right," Schlesinger informed Wicker, "and I can only plead an unconquerable New England bias on the part of the White House staff." He promised that the error would not be repeated. The *Richmond New Leader* trumpeted Schlesinger's apology with the headline: "President Concedes: Virginia Receives Thanksgiving Credit."[12]

True to his word, Schlesinger made sure that JFK did not slight Virginia the following year. On November 5, 1963—seventeen days before his assassination—Kennedy issued a Thanksgiving proclamation, which began: "Over three centuries ago, our forefathers in Virginia and in Massachusetts, far from home in a lonely wilderness, set aside a time of thanksgiving." Previous presidents had not seen fit to mention Virginia's place in the history of Thanksgiving. Virginians were pleased to note that their state was named first, followed by the president's home state of Massachusetts.

During a visit to Berkeley Plantation in 2007, President George W. Bush gave a tip of the hat to its claim on the First Thanksgiving: "The good folks here say that the founders of Berkeley held their celebration before the Pilgrims had even left port," Bush told the crowd. "As you can imagine, this version of events is not very popular up north."[13]

In addition to San Elizario, St. Augustine, and Berkeley Plantation, there are several other claimants to the title of First Thanksgiving.

Palo Duro Canyon, Texas. On May 29, 1541, a large troop of Spanish explorers held a ceremony of thanksgiving in the panhandle of Texas, probably at Palo Duro Canyon, not far from the present-day city of Amarillo. Francisco Vásquez de Coronado had led an army of one thousand five hundred men north from Mexico far up into what is now Texas. They were searching for gold and eventually traveled all the way to Kansas in their quest.

At Palo Duro Canyon, the explorers stopped to give thanks to God. A Franciscan missionary celebrated a thanksgiving Mass, while local people looked on in amazement, according to legend. The priest was Juan de Padilla, who was later killed by Indians, thus becoming one of the first Christian martyrs in the United States.

Fort Caroline, Florida. Next up are French Protestants. On June 30, 1564, a group of Huguenots celebrated a thanksgiving in their new settlement at Fort Caroline on the St. Johns River, near what is now Jacksonville. Like the Pilgrims, they were seeking religious freedom when they fled their homes in Roman Catholic France to establish a colony in the New World. Also like the Pilgrims, they established friendly relations with the local inhabitants, the Timucua Indians.

The Huguenot leader, René Goulaine de Laudonnière, wrote an account of the 1564 Thanksgiving in Florida:

> I commanded a trumpet to be sounded, that, being assembled, we might give God thanks for our favorable and safe arrival. Then we sang a hymn of thanksgiving unto God, beseeching him of His grace to continue his accustomed goodness towards us, his poor servants, and aid us in all enterprises that might turn to His glory and the advancement of our King.

The French would have consumed most of their food supplies during their long voyage across the Atlantic, so it is possible that the meal that followed the Mass was provided largely by the Timucua. The Timucua were excellent hunters, according to the Jacksonville Historical Society, and they also maintained large granaries in which they stored food they had grown, such as corn, beans, and squash. Their diet was rich in seafood, including oysters, shrimp, and mullet, along with the occasional alligator, which they preferred to eat smoked.[14]

The year after the Huguenots gave thanks in Florida, their colony was wiped out by Spanish raiders sent by Philip II. These were the same men, led by General Menéndez, who celebrated a thanksgiving upon their arrival in Florida in 1565. The king had issued orders to "hang and burn the Lutherans," the word "Lutheran" being a catchall Spanish term for Protestants. Menéndez obliged.

Popham Colony, Maine. New England has just one rival to Plymouth for the title of First Thanksgiving. That event took place in 1607, at an English settlement founded where the Kennebec River meets the Atlantic Ocean—about twenty-five miles northeast of what is now the city of Portland. Arriving there in late summer, the Popham Colony settlers built Fort St. George and joined with local Abenaki Indians that autumn for a prayer meeting and feast of local seafood.

The colony of about one hundred Englishmen was named after its main financial backer, Sir John Popham, and his nephew, Captain George Popham, who served as the colony's president. Half the settlers returned to England in December when it became clear that their winter provisions were inadequate. The others followed suit the next year. No one knows why the remaining colonists gave up and went home. Perhaps they didn't want to face another harsh New England winter, or maybe relations with the Indians had soured. There also appears to have been a leadership vacuum after George Popham died in February 1608, and then, several months later, his successor decided to return to England upon learning that he had inherited an estate.

Popham Colony has been called the early American settlement that history forgot. Archeologists found the remnants of the settlement, including Fort St. George, only in 1994, working from a map that had been discovered in a library in Madrid in 1888.[15]

Jamestown, Virginia. In June 1610, the starving colonists of Jamestown held a Thanksgiving prayer service to give thanks for the arrival of an English supply ship carrying desperately needed food. The winter of 1609–1610 had been so severe that most of the colonists died. Fewer than one hundred of the five hundred original colonists survived.

There is one more thanksgiving celebrated by Europeans in the New World that bears mention as one of the earliest recorded in North America. It happened in Canada. The year was 1578, during the third voyage of Martin Frobisher, an English explorer who was seeking the fabled Northwest Passage to the Pacific Ocean. The location of the event was just off the southeast corner of Baffin Island, now part of the province of Nunavut, in the area that would be named Frobisher Bay.

It was summer, but the subarctic weather was fierce, and Frobisher's fleet of fifteen ships had been scattered. On July 31, 1578, after safely sailing past "a great island of ice" at the entrance to the harbor, Frobisher encountered two ships that he feared had been lost. The men "greatly rejoiced" at their "happy meeting." Then they "highly praised God" and, falling to their knees, "gave Him due, humble and hearty thanks." The minister traveling with them "made unto them a godly sermon, exhorting them especially to be thankful to God for their strange and miraculous deliverance in those so dangerous places" and "willed them to enjoy and accept thankfully whatsoever adventure his divine Providence should appoint."[16]

In assessing the challengers for the title of First Thanksgiving, it is important to remember the obvious: The true First Thanksgivings in what became the United States were celebrated not by new arrivals from Europe, but by the indigenous people who had resided in North America for thousands of years. There is no written record of such events, but tribal traditions and ethnological research indicate that Native American tribes practiced thanksgiving rituals at the harvest season as well as at other times of the year. The Green Corn Festival still celebrated by a number of tribes is one example. One Indian authority describes it as a religious ceremony in which the early corn is presented as a sacred offering to the Great Spirit.

Pilgrim Edward Winslow provides an intriguing look at the spiritual beliefs of the Wampanoag and how they gave thanks in his book *Good Newes from New England*, first published in 1624. On his way home to Plymouth after caring for the Wampanoag sachem Massasoit while he was gravely ill, Winslow stopped overnight at the home of another Indian leader, Conbatant, whom he described as a "notable politician, yet full of merry jests."

Winslow and Conbatant hit it off. They enjoyed each other's company and their discussions ranged widely, facilitated by Hobbamock, the Wampanoag who served as the Pilgrims' chief interpreter. At dinner, Conbatant, observing that Winslow bowed his head and spoke some words before and after the meal, asked what he was doing. He was praying, Winslow explained. A theological conversation ensued. Winslow described his Christian beliefs, which, he told Conbatant, dictated how he and his fellow Pilgrims at Plymouth lived their lives. He spoke of the Ten Commandments, of which Conbatant and his men expressed approval—all, that is, except the Seventh, the commandment against adultery, to which they objected on the ground of "too many inconveniences" in a man being tied to one woman. "Whatsoever good things we had, we received from God," who nourishes and strengthens our bodies, Winslow told Conbatant. That is the reason for bowing our heads and offering prayers of thanks before and after we eat, he explained. Conbatant and his men nodded their heads in agreement, saying they believed the same things. "The same power that we called God," Winslow records, "they called *Kiehtan*."[17]

These pre-Plymouth thanksgivings—Spanish, English, Huguenot, Native American—are all historically noteworthy, although none influenced the holiday that Americans celebrate today, except, perhaps, in the sense that they encouraged an attitude of gratitude and reinforced the custom of giving thanks to God. None of the early thanksgivings will supplant our familiar holiday either on the national calendar or in the hearts of Americans. Their significance lies in reminding us of our varied origins, the diversity of religious traditions in our pluralistic history, and the universality of the human wish to give thanks. They, too, are part of the American experience. The common thread among them is a desire to express gratitude to God even in the midst of hardship or misfortune.

Al Borrego of San Elizario could have been speaking for the partisans of all the competing First Thanksgivings when he said, "Our national Thanksgiving is not determined by when it happened. It's based on what it's about."

CHAPTER THREE

America Discovers the Pilgrims

They knew they were pilgrims.
— William Bradford

I t is impossible today to imagine Thanksgiving without the Pilgrims. The two are linked inextricably in the modern imagination. But this wasn't always the case. The Pilgrims didn't take their place at the Thanksgiving table until the nineteenth century.

The holiday we celebrate in late November developed first from the religious days of thanksgiving that were observed in all the American colonies during the seventeenth and eighteenth centuries. Thanksgiving was a day for worship, homecoming, and a grand meal. But the Pilgrims? Who were they? The harvest feast they shared with the Wampanoag Indians in 1621, an event universally known and beloved today, was lost to history for two centuries. It wasn't until long-missing Pilgrim documents were discovered in the nineteenth century that the story of their feast at Plymouth was brought to light.

Those are two roots of our Thanksgiving Day: the religious custom of marking days of thanksgiving, and the Pilgrims' feast with the Wampanoag in 1621. There is also a third root: a now mostly forgotten winter holiday that is celebrated in Plymouth on the anniversary of the day the Pilgrims landed there in 1620. For a glimpse of this holiday, find your way to Plymouth on December 21—but don't plan to sleep late the next morning. Anyone not awake before first light on December 22 can expect to be catapulted from bed at dawn by three blasts of a cannon. Happy Forefathers Day!

If you haven't heard of Forefathers Day, you are not alone. Today it is mostly unknown outside Plymouth, where it is still celebrated with gusto by a small group of enthusiasts at two venerable local organizations. One is the Old Colony Club, whose founders created Forefathers Day in 1769. The other is the Pilgrim Society, which was founded in 1819 to memorialize the Pilgrims.

Long before most of their fellow Plymouth residents are awake on Forefathers Day, members of the Old Colony Club begin celebrating the day. They gather before dawn for an early-morning march to the top of Cole's Hill, where, as the sun comes up, they have an uninterrupted view of Plymouth Harbor and the replica of the *Mayflower* that lies at anchor there. Standing near a statue of the Wampanoag chieftain Massasoit, club members conduct a ceremony of remembrance, after which they fire off a salute on the club's cannon. The Pilgrim Society's celebrations include a festive dinner at which a noteworthy figure delivers an oration on the Pilgrims. These features of the Forefathers Day celebrations—parade, service of remembrance, cannon volley, banquet, oration—have changed very little since they first took shape in the eighteenth century.

In the history of Thanksgiving, Forefathers Day looms large for one important reason: It gave us the Pilgrims—both their designation as "Pilgrims" and a recognition of their importance in American history.

Before the first Forefathers Day was celebrated in 1769, the Pilgrims had fallen into obscurity. Their deeds were receding from memory, overtaken by those of the more successful and better-known Massachusetts Bay Colony, into which Plymouth had been absorbed in 1692. When they were spoken of, the men and women who had arrived on the *Mayflower* were called "First Comers" or "Old Comers" or "First Planters." The name "Pilgrims" didn't come into use until the 1790s, after a preacher employed it in a Forefathers Day sermon, and a poet used it in a Forefathers Day ode. The word itself, however, was first applied to the Plymouth settlers by William Bradford, the longtime governor of the colony. In his description of the settlers' tearful farewell as they departed Holland, he wrote: "They knew they were pilgrims and...lift[ed] up their eyes to the heavens, their dearest country, and quieted their spirits."[1]

Like Thanksgiving, Forefathers Day is a homegrown holiday. It was created in the years leading up to the Revolutionary War, when Americans were seeking heroes and inspirational stories rooted in their own continent and their own New World experiences. For this, they turned to the original settlers of New England, the men and women who had sailed on the *Mayflower*.

As the thirteen colonies trod the path to rebellion, war, and independence, Americans began to see themselves in the Pilgrims. Like the eighteenth-century American revolutionaries, the Pilgrims sought freedom from the tyranny of the English Crown. A century and a half after the *Mayflower* had delivered the Pilgrims to the New World, the heirs of the Pilgrims were prepared to go to war to finish the job their forefathers had begun. They would liberate themselves for good from English oppression.

By the Julian calendar in use at the time in England and its colonies, the small band of Pilgrims from the *Mayflower* arrived at Plymouth on Monday, December 11, 1620. There is an arcane debate about whether that date corresponds to December 21 or December 22 on the Gregorian calendar we use today, and Plymoutheans politely agree to disagree. That's why the Pilgrim Society holds its Forefathers Day dinner on December 21, while the Old Colony Club marks the day on December 22.

The Pilgrims' arrival in Plymouth is often called "the Landing," usually spelled with that grandiose capital letter. Legend has it that the Pilgrims stepped onto the terra firma of the New World by way of a massive boulder on the shoreline. This is the Plymouth Rock that has gained iconic status in American culture. There is, however, no historical evidence to confirm its role in Plymouth's history. Bradford doesn't mention the rock in his monumental history of the founding and early years of the colony, *Of Plymouth Plantation*. Nor does it put in an appearance in the extant letters from the period. Rather, the legend of the rock came to light in 1741 when an elderly townsman by the name of Thomas Faunce, upset that a wharf was going to be built over the boulder, claimed that it had been the stepping stone of the first Pilgrims as they came ashore.

Faunce was not a reliable witness. For one thing, he was ninety-four years old at the time he recounted the story of the rock. No matter how sound his elderly mind may have been or how prodigious his memory, he was relating a story he had heard as a child, three-quarters of a century earlier. Moreover, the story came to him at third hand. He said he had heard about the boulder from his father, who arrived in Plymouth in 1623, three years after the Pilgrims. The elder Faunce told his son that he had learned about the rock from residents who had been passengers on the *Mayflower*.

The logistics of the Landing also make the story of the rock unlikely. As the writer Bill Bryson has observed, "No prudent mariner would try to bring a ship alongside a boulder on a heaving December sea when a sheltered inlet beckoned from nearby."[2]

The story of Plymouth Rock is a myth, but the heroic Landing is not. The small band of Pilgrims who arrived in Plymouth in December 1620 were part of an exploratory party from the *Mayflower* tasked with scouting out locations for a permanent settlement. The *Mayflower* had reached Cape Cod in mid-November and set anchor off the tip of the peninsula in the harbor of what is now Provincetown, Massachusetts.

The English settlers knew that their survival in the New World would depend heavily on their ability to farm, and they quickly determined that the sandy soil of Cape Cod was unsuitable for that purpose. So the scouting party set off to seek a more propitious location. They hoped to settle on a site for their new home before the winter set in.

Eighteen men—Pilgrims and crew—set sail in a small boat called a shallop that had been carried in pieces aboard the *Mayflower* and then assembled at Cape Cod. The men on the shallop were looking for a protected harbor that one of the *Mayflower's* pilots recalled from a fishing expedition he had made several years earlier. The pilot had only a vague recollection of the harbor's location, but he thought he would be able to find it once they were in the area.

By then it was December, and the weather was unpredictable. Soon the shallop and its passengers were caught up in a violent storm—rain, snow, sleet, wind. The shallop's mast snapped in three places and the rudder broke. The little party managed to get their boat ashore and take shelter on what they later discovered was a tiny island.

Mark Twain would later observe that "If you don't like the weather in New England now, wait a few minutes." So it was for the Pilgrims, who woke the next morning to a perfect day. Saturday dawned "fair" and "sunshining," wrote Bradford, who was among the marooned men. The Pilgrims explored the island, dried their clothes, repaired the shallop, and, Bradford tells us, "gave God thanks for His mercies in their manifold deliverances."[3] In some sense, this was the Pilgrims' first thanksgiving on land in the New World.

The following day was Sunday, so the party rested and worshipped.

On Monday, they departed the island and sailed the short distance across the harbor to the place that would become their new home.

Forefathers Day was born in 1769, when seven upstanding men of Plymouth decided to form a social club. Their motives were a mix of the sacred and the profane.

First, the profane: According to the minutes of the club's inaugural meeting, the founders wished to have a private venue where they could gather away from the local hoi polloi. They wanted to be free from "intermixing with the company at the taverns in this town." A "well-regulated club" would increase "the pleasure and happiness of the respective members" and also "conduce to their edification and instruction." They incorporated their new society under the name Old Colony Club.[4]

The new club wasn't just about drinking. It had a higher purpose too, one that the founders considered a sacred duty. The seven original members, proud of their town's history, decided to solemnize the anniversary of the arrival of the Pilgrims by means of an annual celebration. The inaugural Forefathers Day was also known as "Old Colony Day" or the "First Celebration of the Landing of our Forefathers."[5]

Club records provide a detailed account. The first Forefathers Day dinner took place at 2:30 in the afternoon at a local inn. The meal began with an Indian pudding, which was followed by a course of succotash and then one of clams, oysters, and codfish. Next came venison that had been roasted on a jack that the Pilgrims had brought with them on the *Mayflower*. The venison course was followed by "sea fowl"—probably gulls or cormorants—and eels. Dessert was apple pie, cranberry tarts, and cheese.

Succotash—a stew of corn and beans—became the traditional culinary feature of Forefathers Day dinners, as essential to the celebration of that holiday as turkey is to Thanksgiving. The word "succotash" is an Anglicized version of the Narragansett word *sohquttahhash*, whose literal meaning is corn beaten into small pieces. Tradition has it that the Wampanoag taught the Pilgrims how to make succotash.

It is fair to say that succotash is an acquired taste. The author of an 1883 cookbook warns that "strangers are rather shy of this peculiar mixture."[6] At Forefathers Day dinners in Plymouth in the twenty-first century, a tureen of succotash is set out on a table across from the bar during the cocktail hour. Guests are invited to help themselves. The line at the bar is longer.[7]

Toasting is another Forefathers Day tradition. Several toasts were offered at the first Forefathers Day dinner in 1769, including one to those "kings under whose indulgent care this colony has flourished and been protected." According to James Thacher, who wrote an authoritative history of Plymouth that was published in 1835, the group conversed in "an agreeable manner" about "our forefathers." The agreeable manner did not last long, and in 1773 the Old Colony Club folded. Thacher is discreet about the breakup, which was precipitated by disagreement about the most contentious issue of the day: independence for the thirteen colonies. Thacher hints at the acrimony that must have pervaded club events when he writes blandly that "unfortunately, some of the members were attached to the royal interest." In other words, the membership of the Old Colony Club, like the citizens of the thirteen colonies, was sharply divided over whether to toast George III or curse him. Among club members loyal to the Crown was Edward Winslow Jr., a descendant of the Pilgrim of the same name. At the outbreak of war in 1776, the younger Winslow fled to Halifax, Nova Scotia, after fighting at the Battle of Lexington on the side of the British.

But Loyalists were in the minority in Plymouth. By the time the Old Colony Club disbanded in 1773, most Plymoutheans had joined in support of Bostonians' protests against the Crown, and they welcomed the erection of a liberty pole in a place of honor in the town square. As Thacher tells it, they condemned "the tyrannical attempts of the British government to enslave our country," voted to boycott British goods, deplored taxation without their consent, and opposed the British quartering of soldiers in Boston.[8] Forefathers Day celebrations resumed in 1774 under the auspices of the town of Plymouth. A century later, in 1875, the Old Colony Club was revived and took up its early tradition once again.

Forefathers Day reached its zenith of popularity during the nineteenth century, when it was marked by public dinners, orations by distinguished public figures, grand balls, and myriad after-dinner toasts to the Pilgrims, Chief Massasoit, George Washington, the republic, and other patriotic subjects.

An English visitor to Plymouth on Forefathers Day 1824 described the celebrations in an anonymous article in a British journal. The festivities began with a "salute of artillery and a peal from the bells," he wrote. In the church, "a brilliant and venerable assemblage" listened to an anniversary address on "the virtues, disinterestedness and sacrifices of the Pilgrim Fathers." More than five hundred people partook of a dinner at Pilgrim Hall, where dozens of toasts were offered in honor of the Pilgrims and "the devout thanksgivings of two hundred years ago," as well as to the memory of George Washington, to the "spirit of our popular elections," and to that portion of the human race "guilty of a skin not colored like our own." In the evening there was a "splendid" ball and a supper.[9]

Another English visitor, writing about Forefathers Day 1838, was struck by American egalitarianism, which was evident at the celebrations. "There was a great mixture…of classes," he observed. "Every person that can save up the requisite sum of three dollars, and who feels no scruples of a religious nature as to joining in such entertainments, makes a point of attending the annual ball." Nowhere was the egalitarian spirit of the Forefathers Day ball more evident than in the dress of partygoers. Only a dozen or so of the men were attired in "what would be considered a proper ball-dress at home," the Englishman wrote. As for the ladies, the visitor was too bewitched to pay much attention to what they were wearing. The women of Plymouth were "specimens of feminine beauty hardly to be surpassed, I think, in any country in the globe."[10]

In contrast to Thanksgiving, which is a family-centered, homey holiday, Forefathers Day was more masculine, being celebrated in the public sphere in which men circulated. Ambitious politicians made their way to Plymouth to deliver Forefathers Day orations, hoping to catch the public eye. One scholar analogizes the Forefathers Day oration of the nineteenth century to the modern-day, first-in-the-nation New Hampshire presidential primary in that it provided an opportunity for the speakers to attract national attention.[11]

John Quincy Adams, who would become the nation's sixth president in 1825, delivered the Forefathers Day oration in 1802, when he was thirty-five years old. He celebrated the Pilgrims as early democrats and praised the Mayflower Compact—the civil contract by which they consented to be governed—as having laid the ground for the Constitution and America's republican form of government.

The best-known Forefathers Day address was given by Daniel Webster, who delivered a stirring oration at the bicentennial in 1820. Two hundred years ago on this day, "the first scene of our history was laid," he told the crowd.[12] He went on to catalogue the Pilgrims' virtues, which included laying the ground for "more perfect civil liberty" and "a higher degree of religious freedom" than the world had previously known.[13] He lauded their respect for private property and the rule of law. He also used the opportunity to denounce the slave trade in powerful images:

> I hear the sound of the hammer. I see the smoke of the furnace where manacles and fetters are still forged for human limbs. I see the visages of those who by stealth and at midnight labor in this work of hell, foul and dark as may become the artificers of such instruments of misery and torture.[14]

Senator William Seward of New York, a leader of the new Republican Party, made the trek to Plymouth in 1855. His Forefathers Day address praised the Pilgrims as advocates of political equality, freedom of conscience, and "the spirit of freedom, which is the soul of the republic itself." In 1920, the year of the tercentennial, Vice President–elect Calvin Coolidge said of the Pilgrims: "No like body ever cast so great an influence on human history."

The most enthusiastic Forefathers Day celebrations were held in Plymouth and Boston. But as was the case with Thanksgiving, the holiday traveled westward as New Englanders carried it with them across the expanding country. New England Societies in New York City, Philadelphia, Cincinnati, New Orleans, Charleston, Buffalo, Detroit, San Francisco, and other cities also marked the day. Several still do.

Forefathers Day elevated the Pilgrims to the national consciousness and helped to secure their place in American history and, eventually, their association with Thanksgiving. The Pilgrims and their story were widely known by the time the nineteenth century began—and Webster's high-publicity bicentennial speech gave them a further boost.

It took a while longer, however, for this historical thread to be woven into the Thanksgiving story. For that we must look to the discovery of an obscure footnote in a scholarly volume that was published in 1841. James W. Baker calls it the "missing link" between the First Thanksgiving of 1621 and the Thanksgiving holiday that Americans celebrate today. Baker's historical detective work uncovered a believe-it-or-not fact about the First Thanksgiving: Before the 1840s, no published document about the Pilgrims made reference to a thanksgiving or a harvest festival in 1621.[15]

The missing-link footnote appeared in *Chronicles of the Pilgrim Fathers*, a collection of original documents from the early years of Plymouth Colony. Among the entries was a copy of Edward Winslow's 1621 letter in which he described the harvest feast shared by the Pilgrims and the Wampanoag. Winslow's letter had originally been published in London in 1622, in a booklet titled *Mourt's Relation*. But the booklet soon disappeared from circulation, and while its contents had been summarized in subsequent publications, the passage on the First Thanksgiving was not mentioned. In 1820, a copy of *Mourt's Relation* was discovered in Philadelphia, and in 1841, Alexander Young included Winslow's letter in his *Chronicles of the Pilgrim Fathers*. It was the first time since its original publication in 1622 that the complete text of the letter—with the description of the 1621 feast—was published. Young added a footnote, which read: "This was the First Thanksgiving, the harvest festival of New England. On this occasion they no doubt feasted on the wild turkey as well as venison."[16]

The only other eyewitness account of the First Thanksgiving, found in William Bradford's *Of Plymouth Plantation*, made a similar journey before being rediscovered in 1855. After Bradford's death in 1657, the manuscript passed to his family, among them his nephew Nathaniel Morton, who used it as the basis for his influential history of Plymouth. Morton also copied portions into town records. Early in the eighteenth century, the manuscript found its way to Thomas Prince, who referred to it in his 1738 history of New England. Neither Morton nor Prince,

however, mentioned Bradford's account of the First Thanksgiving. After Prince's death, the manuscript was kept in a library in the steeple of
the Old South Meeting House in Boston, where it disappeared during
the Revolutionary War when British troops occupied the church. The
trail then went cold for nearly a century until, in the 1850s, it turned up
in the library of the bishop of London—presumably having been carried to England by British soldiers who had looted the Meeting House
during the war. When the complete text of Bradford's *Of Plymouth
Plantation* was finally published in 1855, it included the passage describing what came to be considered the original Thanksgiving celebration.
It was the first time that passage appeared in print.[17]

Baker says that Alexander Young's 1841 identification of the 1621
event as the "First Thanksgiving" was slow to gain traction with the
public. The Thanksgiving holiday was already well established, Baker
notes, and had "developed a substantial historical tradition quite inde-
pendent of the Pilgrims."[18]

Still, by the 1860s, popular culture had enthusiastically adopted
the Pilgrims' Thanksgiving story, which was being retold in painting
and song and literature. The artistic renderings sometimes contained
more fiction than fact, but the basic story came through loud and
strong, and by the end of the nineteenth century, the Pilgrims' place
in Thanksgiving was here to stay. The poets and the painters and the
novelists may not have gotten all of the details right, but the essence of
the story of the First Thanksgiving was right on target.

CHAPTER FOUR

George Washington Sets the Stage

Both Houses of Congress have by their joint Committee requested me to recom-mend to the People of the United States a day of public thanksgiving and prayer.
— President George Washington

I t is hard to imagine Americans' favorite holiday as a source of political controversy. But such was the case in 1789, the year of our first Thanksgiving as a nation.

The controversy began on September 25 in New York City, then the seat of the government of the new United States of America. The venue was the inaugural session of the United States Congress. The senators and representatives had been meeting since March 4 at Federal Hall in lower Manhattan and were about to take a well-deserved break.

The first federal Congress, which ran from 1789 to 1791, is often called the most important and productive Congress in American history. It was charged with interpreting and implementing the new Constitution, a job that included fleshing out the structure of government as outlined in that document and passing enabling legislation. It had been a busy half year. One of Congress's first tasks was to count the electoral votes sent in by the states and certify the elections of President George Washington and Vice President John Adams. Washington had no challenger and was elected unanimously. He took the oath of office on April 30 on the steps of Federal Hall at the corner of Wall and Nassau streets. Adams, who won a majority of the electoral votes, had already taken office on April 21.

In its first six months, Congress created the departments of State, War, and the Treasury. It defined the structure and jurisdiction of the federal courts, establishing the Supreme Court, the circuit courts, and the federal district courts. It debated and approved the ten constitutional amendments that, upon ratification by the states, would become the Bill of Rights.

Finally, on Friday, September 25, 1789, Congress was about to recess when Representative Elias Boudinot of New Jersey rose to introduce a resolution.[1] He asked the House to create a joint committee with the Senate to "wait upon the President of the United States, to request that he would recommend to the people of the United States a day of public thanksgiving and prayer to be observed by acknowledging, with grateful hearts, the many signal favors of Almighty God." Boudinot made special reference to the Constitution, which had been ratified by the requisite two-thirds of the states in 1788. A day of public thanksgiving, he believed, would allow Americans to express gratitude to God for the "opportunity peaceably to establish a Constitution of government for their safety and happiness."

In proposing a congressional resolution on a day of thanksgiving,

Boudinot was drawing on a tradition established by the Continental Congress during the Revolutionary War, when it proclaimed days of national thanksgiving. In 1777, the year of its first Thanksgiving proclamation, the Continental Congress asked the Almighty "to smile upon us in the prosecution of a just and necessary war" and to "inspire our commanders both by land and sea." The proclamation of 1781 expressed thanks for the Articles of Confederation, which had been signed by all the states. In 1783, at war's end, the Continental Congress proclaimed thanks for "the cessation of all hostilities by land and sea" and for having "their freedom, sovereignty and independence ultimately acknowledged by the king of Great Britain."

Boudinot's resolution sparked a vigorous debate. The opposition was led by two members from South Carolina, Aedanus Burke and Thomas Tudor Tucker. Both disagreed with Boudinot on the proper role of the executive branch: Boudinot wanted a strong central government, while the South Carolinians favored a weak one. Another source of difference was religion. Boudinot was a devout Presbyterian—trustee of the Presbyterian-founded College of New Jersey (now Princeton University) and later the first president of the American Bible Society. The religious affiliations of Burke and Tucker are not known, but both raised concerns about the implications for religion in the new constitutional order.

Burke, who had been born in Ireland, objected to Boudinot's resolution on the grounds that a day of thanksgiving was too "European." He "did not like this mimicking of European customs, where they made a mere mockery of thanksgivings." His argument was somewhat obscure. In Europe, he explained, both parties at war frequently sang the

Te Deum, a hymn of praise sung in the Catholic Mass. Burke apparently was objecting to what he viewed as the hypocrisy of both the victor and the loser singing a hymn of thanksgiving.

Tucker raised two objections. The first had to do with the separation of powers as enumerated in the new federal Constitution. Tucker argued that the federal government did not have the authority to proclaim days of thanksgiving; that was among the powers left to individual state governments. "Why should the President direct the people to do what, perhaps, they have no mind to do?" he asked. "If a day of thanksgiving must take place," he said, "let it be done by the authority of the several States."

Tucker's second reservation had to do with separation of church and state. Proclaiming a day of thanksgiving "is a religious matter," he argued, "and, as such, proscribed to us." The Bill of Rights would not be ratified until 1791, but Congress had just approved the wording of the First Amendment, and the debate about the proper role of religion was fresh in everyone's mind. The First Amendment prohibits any law respecting an establishment of religion.

It fell to a New Englander to stand up in support of Thanksgiving. Connecticut's Roger Sherman praised Boudinot's resolution as "a laudable one in itself." It also was "warranted by a number of precedents" in the Bible, he said, "for instance the solemn thanksgivings and rejoicings which took place in the time of Solomon, after the building of the temple."

In the end, the Thanksgiving resolution passed—the precise vote is not recorded—and the House appointed a committee made up of

Representatives Boudinot, Sherman, and Peter Silvester of New York. The resolution moved to the Senate, which quickly approved it. Senators William Samuel Johnson of Connecticut and Ralph Izard of South Carolina were appointed to the joint committee.

On September 28, the senators reported that the joint committee had delivered the congressional resolution to the president. Five days later, on October 3, George Washington issued his now-famous Thanksgiving proclamation. He designated Thursday, November 26, 1789 as "a day of public thanksgiving and prayer."

Washington opened his proclamation by asserting that it is "the duty of all Nations to acknowledge the providence of Almighty God" and "to obey his will, to be grateful for his benefits, and humbly to implore his protection and favor." He asked the American people to observe a day of thanksgiving and prayer by "acknowledging with grateful hearts the many signal favors of Almighty God especially by affording them an opportunity peaceably to establish a form of government for their safety and happiness."

He went on to ask Americans to render their "sincere and humble thanks" to God for "his kind care and protection of the People of this Country previous to their becoming a Nation," for the Almighty's care "in the course and conclusion of the late war," and for the "great degree of tranquility, union, and plenty, which we have since enjoyed." He offered thanks for the "peaceable and rational manner" in which Americans were able to "establish constitutions of government for our safety and happiness" and for the "civil and religious liberty with which we are blessed." And he spoke of "all the great and various favors which [God] hath been pleased to confer upon us."

He concluded by beseeching God "to pardon our national and other transgressions"—transgressions that he did not enumerate. He asked God to "render our national government a blessing to all the people, by constantly being a Government of wise, just, and constitutional laws, discreetly and faithfully executed and obeyed."

Washington sent a copy of his proclamation to each of the thirteen governors along with a kind of cover note known as his "Circular to the Governors of the States." He wrote: "I do myself the honor to enclose to your Excellency a Proclamation for a general Thanksgiving which I must request the favor of you to have published and made known in your State in the way and manner that shall be more agreeable to you."[2]

Note that the president used the words "request" and "favor" when asking the governors to distribute his proclamation. Similarly, Congress's joint resolution had asked Washington to "recommend" to the "people of the United States" a day of thanksgiving. This was the first presidential proclamation, and Washington's language suggests that he understood that it did not carry the force of law.

In the event, the proclamation was well heeded. According to the editors of *The Papers of George Washington*, compiled by the University of Virginia, Thanksgiving Day was "widely celebrated throughout the nation."[3] Newspapers around the country published the president's proclamation, and states announced plans for public functions in honor of the day. Religious services were held, and churches solicited donations for the indigent.

Washington himself sent twenty-five dollars to a pastor in New

York City, requesting that the funds be "applied towards relieving the poor of the Presbyterian Churches," in the words of his secretary, Tobias Lear. "The President of the United States has directed me to send it to you, requesting that you will be so good as to put it into the way of answering the charitable purpose for which it is intended."[4]

Washington was keenly aware of his historic role as a model for future presidents. Not long after taking office he remarked: "I walk on untrodden ground. There is scarcely any part of my conduct which may not be hereafter drawn into precedent."[5] His Thanksgiving proclamation of 1789 set the standard for similar proclamations by future presidents, a list that includes James Madison and then every president since Abraham Lincoln.

There is a notable absence in the list of presidents who issued Thanksgiving proclamations: Thomas Jefferson. The third president of the United States pointedly declined to do so.

Jefferson had principled reasons for refusing to issue such a proclamation, which he explained in a letter to a New York City minister by the name of Samuel Miller, dated January 23, 1808.[6] The Reverend Miller had written the president soliciting his views on whether his constitutional powers extended to naming a day of national thanksgiving and prayer. Jefferson wrote in reply that he did "not consider [himself] authorized" to issue a Thanksgiving proclamation because the Constitution prohibits a president from "intermeddling with religious institutions, their doctrines, discipline, or exercises." He quoted the First Amendment, which he described as "the provision that no law shall be made respecting the establishment, or free exercise, of religion."

Naming a day of thanksgiving and prayer was a religious matter, he informed the minister, and therefore not an appropriate role for the federal government. "Every religious society has a right to determine for itself the times for these exercises, & the objects proper for them, according to their own particular tenets; and this right can never be safer than in their own hands, where the constitution has deposited it."

Jefferson offered a second reason for his decision. Under the Constitution, he wrote, the authority to issue a Thanksgiving proclamation rightly belongs to the states, not the federal government. The Constitution reserves to the states the powers not delegated to the central government. "Certainly no power to prescribe any religious exercise, or to assume authority in religious discipline, has been delegated to the general government. It must then rest with the states."

The remainder of Jefferson's letter resembles a dialogue with himself, as he raises arguments supporting a presidential Thanksgiving proclamation and then refutes them.

Jefferson notes that a presidential Thanksgiving proclamation is just a recommendation, not a requirement. There is no penalty attached to those who disregard a presidential proclamation—no fine or imprisonment. So why not do it? He answers his own question by observing that a Thanksgiving proclamation carries the authority of the president of the United States and therefore has influence on public opinion. He concludes that it is inappropriate for a president to urge the public to mark a day of thanksgiving. Second, he refers to "the practice of my predecessors," meaning George Washington and John Adams. Washington issued Thanksgiving proclamations and Adams called for days of fasting and prayer. Why shouldn't Jefferson carry on this presidential tradition? Jefferson argues that his two predecessors were unduly influenced by "the example of state executives"—that is, governors—who had designated thanksgiving and fast days. The presidents, he writes, issued their proclamations "without due examination." If they had considered the matter more thoughtfully, they "would have discovered that what might be a right in a state government was a violation of that right when assumed by another."

Although he does not mention it in the letter, it bears noting that Jefferson was one of those state executives who issued Thanksgiving proclamations. In 1777, when he was governor of Virginia, he called for "a day of public and solemn thanksgiving and prayer to Almighty God, earnestly recommending to all the good people of this commonwealth, to set apart the said day for those purposes." Governor Jefferson's proclamation was in response to a request by the Continental Congress and had been approved by the Virginia legislature.

Finally, in his letter to the Reverend Miller, Jefferson refers to his own conscience. "Every one must act according to the dictates of his own reason," he writes, and "mine tells me that civil powers alone have been given to the President of the U.S. and no authority to direct the religious exercises of his constituents."

Jefferson's arguments against presidential Thanksgiving proclamations have not held up in the succeeding centuries. Even in his time, when Thanksgiving was explicitly a day of prayer on which religious services were widely observed, a presidential proclamation that did not mention a specific religion was unlikely to have been deemed unconstitutional. The First Amendment does not bar the executive branch from mentioning God.

Since 1941, the date of our annual Thanksgiving celebration has been set by law as the fourth Thursday in November. The holiday would take place whether or not a president chose to issue a proclamation. Even so, presidents continue the tradition of issuing annual Thanksgiving proclamations. With Washington's original proclamation serving as an unofficial template, the language and content of presidential Thanksgiving proclamations bear striking similarities from the eighteenth century to the twenty-first.

Proclamations give thanks to God, who is named in a variety of creative and often poetic ways, as well as with more familiar appellations:

* "the Bestower of Every Good Gift" (John Adams, 1798)
* "the Great Disposer of Events of the Destiny of Nations... the same Divine Author of Every Good and Perfect Gift" (James Madison, 1815)
* "Most High God" (Abraham Lincoln, 1863)
* "the Supreme Author from whom such blessings flow" (Ulysses S. Grant, 1869)
* "the Father of All Mercies" (Grant, 1876)

* "the Great Ruler of Times and Seasons and Events" (Rutherford Hayes, 1877)
* "the Giver of All Good" (Chester Arthur, 1883)
* "Ruler of the Universe" (Grover Cleveland, 1886)
* "the Most High...the Giver of Good" (Theodore Roosevelt, 1902)
* "Almighty God" (Woodrow Wilson, 1917)
* "the Chief Magistrate" (Herbert Hoover, 1929)
* "the Father of us all" (Franklin Roosevelt, 1941)
* "Almighty Providence" (Harry S. Truman, 1945)
* "Divine Providence" (Richard Nixon, 1972)
* "the Almighty" (Ronald Reagan, 1987)
* "the loving Source of all Life and Liberty" (George H. W. Bush, 1990)
* "One greater than ourselves" (George W. Bush, 2001)

A partial exception to the long list of God-centered Thanksgiving proclamations was the one delivered by Barack Obama in 2009. That year, the president was criticized for mentioning God only indirectly. The sole reference to God came when he quoted Washington's reference to "Almighty God." The next year, God was back. Obama's 2010 proclamation said: "...we lift up our hearts in gratitude to God for our many blessings."

Many of the Thanksgiving proclamations contain prayers or language that is prayerlike. In his proclamation of 1942—the first Thanksgiving after America's entry into World War II—FDR included the complete text of the Twenty-third Psalm, which begins, "The Lord is my Shepherd, I shall not want." In addition, he named Thanksgiving Day and New Year's Day as days of prayer.

Another traditional feature of Thanksgiving proclamations is that they express gratitude for American freedoms—religious and civil—and for the American system of government. A large number reference the Founders. In 1876, the centennial of the founding of the United States, Grant spoke of how the nation "has been enabled to fulfill the purpose of its founders in offering an asylum to the people of every race, securing civil and religious liberty to all within its borders, and meting out to every individual alike justice and equality before the law." One hundred twenty years later, Bill Clinton called on Americans in 1996 to "reawaken ourselves and our neighbors and our communities to the genius of our founders in daring to build the world's first constitutional democracy on the foundation of trust and thanks to God."

In 1905, Theodore Roosevelt became the first president to refer directly to the Pilgrims in a Thanksgiving proclamation, when he spoke of the privations of the "first settlers." The Pilgrims feature in many subsequent proclamations. Gerald Ford exhorted Americans in 1974 to be "worthy heirs of the Pilgrim spirit."

Ronald Reagan was the first president to mention Native Americans and their ancient traditions of giving thanks, which "antedated those of the new Americans." His 1984 proclamation quoted a Seneca Indian prayer: "Give it your thought, that with one mind we may now give thanks to Him our Creator." Obama paid tribute in 2011 to the Wampanoag "for generously extending their knowledge of local game and agriculture to the Pilgrims." He urged Americans to "take this time to remember the ways that the First Americans have enriched our Nation's heritage."

Numerous Thanksgiving proclamations have recapped the top news of the year—war, natural disaster, the death of a president:

★ In 1900, William McKinley offered thanks that many Americans had survived the Boxer Rebellion in China, where foreigners had been murdered. "The lives of our official representatives and many of our people in China have been marvelously preserved," the president said.

★ The following year, President Theodore Roosevelt's proclamation acknowledged the nation's grief over McKinley's assassination in Buffalo by a Polish-American anarchist. "The season is night," TR wrote.

★ In 1917, the United States entered World War I, after President Woodrow Wilson's failure to keep the country neutral. In his Thanksgiving proclamation of that year, Wilson spoke solemnly of Americans' duties: "A new light shines about us. The great duties of a new day awaken a new and greater national spirit in us. We shall never again be divided or wonder what stuff we are made of."

★ In 1923, Calvin Coolidge eulogized the late President Warren Harding, who had died that year. He called on Americans to remember those who perished in the great Tokyo earthquake. That disaster, he wrote, "replenished the charitable impulse" of the United States.

★ Harry Truman gave thanks in 1945 for the Allied victory in World War II that summer: "In this year of our victory, absolute and final, over German fascism and Japanese militarism; in this time of peace so long awaited, which we are determined with all the United Nations to make permanent; on this day of our abundance, strength, and achievement; let us give thanks to Almighty Providence for these exceeding blessings."

★ At the height of the Cold War, in 1961, Kennedy expressed gratitude for, among other things, "the strength of our arms" and "our determination to stand firmly for what we believe to be right and to resist mightily what we believe to be base."

★ In 2001, just weeks after the terrorist attacks of September 11, George W. Bush asked Americans to "let our thanksgiving be revealed in the compassionate support we render to our fellow citizens who are grieving unimaginable loss."

Presidents have often used their Thanksgiving proclamations to offer moral lessons and uphold civic virtues such as patriotism, generosity, and compassion.

★ In 1882, Chester Arthur asked Americans to set aside Thanksgiving Day as a "special occasion for deeds of kindness and charity to the suffering and the needy, so that all who dwell within the land may rejoice and be glad in this season of national thanksgiving."

★ Teddy Roosevelt gave thanks in 1906 for the nation's prosperity, then warned about the dangers of worshipping Mammon: "Material well-being, indispensable though it is, can never be anything but the foundation of true national greatness and happiness. If we build nothing upon this foundation, then our national life will be meaningless and empty as a house where only the foundation has been laid."

★ In 2011, Barack Obama spoke of "the simple gifts that sustain us" and called on Americans to "pay them forward."

Almost every proclamation ends by noting the number of years since the promulgation of the Declaration of Independence in 1776.

George Washington set another precedent for Thanksgiving proclamations: nonsectarianism. His 1789 proclamation was religiously inclusive. He spoke of God—the first line described "the duty of all Nations to acknowledge the providence of Almighty God"—but he made no reference to a specific religion. He spoke instead of "the civil and religious liberty with which we are blessed."

His 1795 Thanksgiving proclamation was even more explicitly ecumenical. "I, George Washington, President of the United States, do recommend to all Religious Societies and Denominations...to set apart and observe...a Day of Public Thanksgiving and Praise."

Washington's religious beliefs have been the subject of speculation. Was he a deist? Was he a Christian? No one, however, doubts his commitment to religious freedom. He was baptized into the Church of England, which became the Episcopal Church after the Revolution. During the first Continental Congress in Philadelphia, he attended Anglican, Catholic, and Quaker worship services. At the time of his first Thanksgiving proclamation, as we saw, he donated money to the Presbyterian Church.

When he was hiring workers for his home at Mount Vernon, Washington wrote to his agent: "If they be good workmen, they may be from Asia, Africa, or Europe; they may be Mohammedans [Muslims], Jews, or Christians of any sect, or they may be Atheists." In his letter to the Hebrew Congregation of Newport, Rhode Island, in 1790, he famously wrote about religious tolerance: "May the Children of the Stock of Abraham, who dwell in this land, continue to merit and enjoy the good will of the other Inhabitants; while every one shall sit in safety under his own vine and figtree, and there shall be none to make him afraid."

Nearly every future president would follow Washington's example in using ecumenical language in his Thanksgiving proclamations. (Exceptions were Grover Cleveland, whose 1896 proclamation referenced Christ, and William McKinley, whose 1900 proclamation referred to "Christian charity.") When it came to proclamations in individual states, however, not all governors were so wise.

In 1844, the Jews of Charleston, South Carolina, refused to celebrate Thanksgiving in protest of a proclamation issued by a governor who did not follow Washington's inclusive example. On September 9 of that year, Governor James Hammond named Thursday, October 3 as a day of thanksgiving and prayer. His proclamation began with a reference to "all Christian nations," and went on to "invite and exhort our citizens of all denominations to assemble at their respective places of worship, to offer up their devotions to God their Creator, and his Son Jesus Christ, the Redeemer of the world." The Jews and other non-Christians of South Carolina were excluded from this call to worship on Thanksgiving.

The Jewish community of Charleston is one of the oldest in the nation, and in 1844 it was also one of the largest. There had been Jews in the Carolina Colony since the seventeenth century, attracted by a colonial constitution that granted freedom of religion to all settlers. The "Fundamental Constitutions of Carolina," written in large part by John Locke in 1669, specifically embraced "Jews, heathens, and dissenters." The first Jew to be elected to high public office in the American colonies was Francis Salvador, having been elected to the General Assembly of South Carolina in 1774, and then to the revolutionary Provincial Congress, which set forth the colonists' grievances against the British Crown. Salvador was also the first Jewish American to die in the Revolutionary War.

In response to Hammond's Thanksgiving proclamation, more than one hundred Jews of Charleston signed a letter of protest. They called the language and spirit of the proclamation "unusual" and "offensive." The Israelites of Charleston, they wrote, "in common with all others of the human family, have bowed their heads in humble submission beneath the chastening rod of their Creator, and in their turn, have also had cause, gratefully to acknowledge bounteous blessings bestowed by His beneficent hand." They asked the governor: "What must have been their emotions when they found themselves *excluded* by your Proclamation, from the general thanksgiving and prayer of the occasion?" The Charleston Jews requested an apology.

The governor's reply only made matters worse. "I have always thought it a settled matter that I lived in a Christian land," he stated. At the time he wrote the proclamation, he said, "it did not occur to me, that there might be Israelites, Deists, Atheists, or any other class of persons in the State who denied the divinity of Jesus Christ." But even if it had occurred to him, he went on to say, he would not have changed the language: "I have no apology to make for it now."

The Charleston Jews formed a committee to compose a public report on Hammond's letter, which they sent to the *Charleston Mercury*.[7] By then it was November and Hammond's term in office was nearing an end. On December 7, he was succeeded by William Aiken Jr. One of Aiken's first acts as governor was to issue a new Thanksgiving proclamation. It contained no references to Christianity.

Governor Aiken, it would seem, was familiar with the tradition of religiously inclusive Thanksgiving proclamations—a tradition started in 1789 by President Washington.

CHAPTER FIVE

Thanksgiving's Godmother

*From this year, 1847, henceforth and forever, so long as the Union endures,
the last Thursday in November [should] be the Day set apart by every
State for its annual Thanksgiving.* —Sarah Josepha Hale

By the time the Civil War began on April 12, 1861, just about every
state had established an annual day of thanksgiving for the purpose
of expressing gratitude for general blessings. The holiday was celebrated
by a day off from work, attendance at religious services, and usually a
festive gathering at home. The classic New England feast made its way to
many parts of the country, though it caught on slowly in the South. But
even in places where turkey and cranberries were missing, Thanksgiving
Day was recognizable as the holiday we celebrate today: a time to suspend
ordinary activities for the purpose of pausing to take stock of personal
blessings as well as our collective blessings as Americans.

The date for Thanksgiving Day was set by individual governors,
who sometimes coordinated but usually didn't. The result was that

while most states celebrated in November, a few marked the day in October or even early December. Meanwhile, pioneers carried Thanksgiving with them to the frontier territories.

In the early years of the Civil War, Presidents Abraham Lincoln and Jefferson Davis each issued proclamations appointing days of thanksgiving for military victories. These were not in the spirit of Washington's 1789 proclamation of a thanksgiving for general blessings. Rather, they harked back to the Thanksgiving proclamations made by colonial leaders in the seventeenth century to celebrate victories over the Indians, the Continental Congress's Thanksgiving proclamations during the Revolutionary War, and President James Madison's Thanksgiving proclamations during and at the conclusion of the War of 1812.

The Davis and Lincoln proclamations were nonsectarian. They made reference to God—"the Sovereign Disposer of events" (Davis) and "the Lord of Hosts" (Lincoln)—but unlike the Thanksgiving proclamations sometimes issued by governors, they were not Christianized. Perhaps the two presidents were following the example of Washington, or perhaps they were offering a nod of respect to their non-Christian populations. Jews fought on both sides during the Civil War.

The first wartime proclamation was issued by Davis in the fall of 1861. The war was in its first year and the Confederacy had the upper hand. In a proclamation dated October 31, 1861, Davis expressed thanks for the Confederate victories and warned of battles to come. He called for a day of national humiliation and prayer—not a day of thanksgiving—to be held throughout the Confederacy on Friday, November 15.

In April 1862, it was Lincoln's turn. The president issued a proclamation following military victories on the Union side. He spoke of battles won by the Union's "land and naval forces engaged in suppressing an internal rebellion" and called on Northerners to give thanks for the victories. Reflecting on the widespread suffering the war had brought, he asked citizens to pray for those "who have been brought into affliction by the casualties and calamities of sedition and civil war." He did not set aside a separate day of thanksgiving. Rather, he urged citizens to give thanks "at their next weekly assemblages in their accustomed places of public worship."

Later that year, it was Davis's turn again. He issued a proclamation of thanks for Confederate victories over the Union army. "On the very day on which our forces were led to victory on the Plains of Manassas, in Virginia," he wrote, "the same Almighty arm assisted us to overcome our enemies at Richmond, in Kentucky." Thus, "at one and the same time, have two great hostile armies been stricken down, and the wicked designs of their armies been set at naught." He set a day of thanksgiving and worship for Thursday, September 18, 1862.

The final thanksgiving for a military victory was proclaimed by Lincoln, when he named Thursday, August 6, 1863 as a day of "national thanksgiving, praise, and prayer." It was a month after the Battle of Gettysburg. A Union victory in the war was in sight, the president said. It had pleased the Almighty "to give the Army and the Navy of the United States victories on land and on the sea so signal and so effective as to furnish reasonable grounds for augmented confidence that the Union of these States will be maintained, their Constitution preserved, and their peace and prosperity permanently restored."

Lincoln's and Davis's proclamations were of course aimed at their own populations—Northerners in Lincoln's case and Southerners in that of Davis. The opposing side was the enemy. Which made what came next all the more remarkable.

Less than two months after the North marked Lincoln's appointed day of thanksgiving for the Union victory at Gettysburg, the president did something surprising: He ordered a second, much different, day of thanksgiving. It was not called for the purpose of giving thanks for a military victory. Rather, it was to acknowledge and give thanks to God for the nation's—the entire nation's—general blessings. This was the first time since Washington led the nation that a president proclaimed a national day of general thanksgiving.

Lincoln's opening sentence set the tone: "The year that is drawing toward its close has been filled with the blessings of fruitful fields and healthful skies." This was an extraordinary way to characterize the year 1863, an exceptionally bloody one for Americans. The Battle of Gettysburg set a new standard for suffering; the Union lost 27 percent of its fighting men, the Confederacy lost 37 percent. Death, suffering, and grief were ever-present. As a Northerner or a Southerner reflected on the year that was ending, "fruitful fields and healthful skies" were unlikely to be the first things that sprang to mind.

Lincoln went on to catalog the blessings for which all Americans could be grateful. Even "in the midst of a civil war of unequaled severity and magnitude," he wrote, the nation remained at peace with foreign countries, its borders were expanding, its population was growing, and its farms, industry, and mines were producing. Lincoln was reminding Americans that the war would eventually end. He was asking them to look beyond the current horrors to a better day, when the country "is permitted to expect continuance of years with large increase of freedom." It was a profoundly hopeful message, reminding the American people of the nation's capacity for renewal.

In his Thanksgiving proclamation, Lincoln spoke not as commander in chief of the Union forces but as president of the entire divided nation, North and South. He made no reference to battles or victories or rebels or enemies. Rather, the president spoke of "the whole American people." He called on every American to celebrate this general Thanksgiving "with one heart and one voice."

Lincoln set Thanksgiving Day for the last Thursday of November, following Washington's example and setting the norm for the future. His 1863 proclamation was also the first in the unbroken string of annual Thanksgiving proclamations by every subsequent president. It is regarded as the beginning of our national Thanksgiving holiday.

To understand how the nation coalesced around the idea of an annual national Thanksgiving, it is necessary to examine the remarkable life of the woman who made it happen. She used her position as editor of the most popular magazine of the pre–Civil War era to conduct a years-long campaign for a national Thanksgiving holiday. She is often called the godmother of Thanksgiving. Her name was Sarah Josepha Hale.

Hale's name won't be found in many books of United States history. Nor will it be on standard lists of the country's great editors or trailblazing feminists, though she was both. When her name comes up, it is usually in the context of her role in bringing about our national Thanksgiving holiday, or her authorship of the children's poem "Mary Had a Little Lamb." But her accomplishments extend well beyond those achievements.

Hale was an author, editor, social reformer, abolitionist and, above all, relentless advocate of women's rights, especially the right to an education. In the words of her biographer Ruth E. Finley, "Not a month passed during her entire half-century of editorship but that Sarah Hale proclaimed the gospel of equal education, equal economic rights, equal recognition under the law, and equal professional opportunity for women."[1]

A partial list of Hale's achievements on behalf of women includes leading the fight for property rights for married women, campaigning for women to be welcome as teachers in public schools, supporting medical education for women, creating the first day-care center for small children and the first public playground, founding a society dedicated to increasing the wages of working women, and helping to found Vassar College, the first college for women. She invented the term "domestic science" as part of her effort to elevate the status of housekeeping.

She was also a prolific writer, author of seven volumes of poetry, six works of fiction, several books on cooking and housekeeping, and a reference book of nine hundred pages about women in history. In addition, she edited more than two dozen books, including poetry anthologies and collections of letters.[2]

Sarah Josepha Buell was born in 1788 in the village of Newport, New Hampshire, to a father who had fought in the Revolutionary War and a mother who placed a high value on education for her daughters as well as her sons. Hale was well educated for a woman of her time, thanks first to her mother and later to her brother and her husband.

There was no school in town, so the Buell children were home-schooled, with their mother as their teacher. In an era when girls did not go to college, Hale received the equivalent of a college education from her elder brother, Horatio, who attended Dartmouth College in nearby Hanover. On visits home, Horatio would teach Sarah what he had learned in his classes at Dartmouth. "To my brother Horatio," she wrote many years later, "I owe what knowledge I have of Latin, of the higher branches of mathematics, and of mental philosophy. He often regretted that I could not, like himself, have the privilege of a college education."[3]

Hale's education continued when, at the relatively late age of twenty-five, she married a New Hampshire lawyer by the name of David Hale. Husband and wife had a routine of nightly study. They would sit together in their sitting room every evening from eight o'clock to ten o'clock reading the classics, studying language and the sciences, and examining the prose style of the great English writers. "In this manner," Hale explained, "we studied French, Botany, then an almost new science in the country...and obtained some knowledge of Mineralogy, Geology, etc., besides pursuing a long and instructive course of reading."[4]

When David Hale died of pneumonia in 1822, Sarah was thirty-four years old. She was left with four children, a fifth on the way, and no means of support. Her late husband's friends in the Masons first set her up in a millinery shop, needlework being one of the few jobs open to respectable women. It failed. They also backed the publication, in 1823, of her first book, a collection of poetry.

In 1827, Hale's life changed dramatically with the publication of her antislavery novel, *Northwood: A Tale of New England*. The book was a bestseller in the United States and went on to be published in London, a rare honor for an American writer. *Northwood's* success brought the author to the attention of a publishing house in Boston that offered her the editorship of a new magazine for women. In January 1828, at the age of thirty-nine, Hale moved to Boston to become editor of *Ladies' Magazine*. It was the start of a journalism career that would last for half a century.

Hale's work at *Ladies' Magazine* caught the eye of Louis Godey, publisher of *Godey's Lady's Book* in Philadelphia. In 1837, Godey bought *Ladies' Magazine*, merged it with *Godey's Lady's Book*, and installed Hale as editor of the new national monthly magazine. Godey had purchased the Boston magazine because he wanted Hale to edit his own periodical and he knew he couldn't get her without first obtaining the magazine for which she worked. Hale would spend the next forty years as the editor of *Godey's Lady's Book*.

At *Godey's*, Hale set out to publish American authors writing on American themes, as she had done at *Ladies' Magazine* in Boston. This approach contrasted with other popular magazines of the day, which typically reprinted articles they had pirated from English publications. Godey and Hale believed there was a market for a national women's magazine that focused on American culture. Godey was willing to pay for original copy, and Hale lined up writers such as Harriet Beecher Stowe, Nathaniel Hawthorne, Washington Irving, and Edgar Allan Poe, who described her as "a lady of fine genius and masculine energy and ability."

Hale's interest in American culture extended to everyday aspects of American life too—food, fashion, manners, childrearing, and running a household. In addition to the literature it published, *Godey's Lady's Book* provided readers with practical information aimed at its largely middle-class readers, such as housekeeping tips, sheet music for the piano, sewing patterns, and the hand-tinted fashion plates for which the magazine became renowned. Hale introduced a recipes section, which may have been the first of its kind in an American women's magazine, and she invited readers to contribute their own recipes.

Under her editorship, *Godey's Lady's Book* became the most widely read periodical in the United States on the eve of the Civil War. Circulation rose from ten thousand subscribers in 1837, when she became editor, to one hundred fifty thousand in 1860.[5] The pass-along rate—as one household passed an issue along to a neighboring household—boosted the readership several times higher. It reached into most parts of the expanding nation. One-third of its circulation was in the South.

The magazine and its "editress," as Hale liked to be called, became influential style setters. For example, the publication in 1850 of an engraving of Queen Victoria and Prince Albert standing in front of their Christmas tree at Windsor Castle helped spread the custom of Christmas trees in the United States. But it was Thanksgiving where Hale's influence would be the most profound.

Thanksgiving Day, a homegrown holiday, fit into Hale's mission of focusing on Americana in her magazine. She saw Thanksgiving as a patriotic occasion along with the Fourth of July and Washington's Birthday, two national holidays that were born of the American experience. She also saw Thanksgiving, with its emphasis on family reunions and a special meal, as falling into the feminine sphere. It reflected, too, what she saw as the generous spirit of the American people.

Godey's Lady's Book was a powerful platform, and Hale used every feature of the magazine—editorials, recipes, short stories—to encourage the celebration of Thanksgiving in all corners of the expanding country. Starting in the 1840s, she employed her monthly column, "Editors' Table," to publish an impassioned series of editorials on Thanksgiving. Her goal was to have Thanksgiving Day established as a national holiday and observed on a uniform date throughout the country.

George Washington had selected the last Thursday in November as the date for the first national Thanksgiving in 1789, so that was the date Hale chose. In the 1850s, after observing the wide variation in the dates that governors had selected for their state Thanksgivings, she flirted with the idea of holding Thanksgiving on the third Thursday of the month. That might be a more suitable date, she wrote, since it was the approximate middle point between the dates chosen by governors the previous year. The third-Thursday notion didn't take flight, however, and she soon went back to pushing for Thanksgiving on the last Thursday of November.

Hale kept track of where and when the holiday was celebrated. In 1847, she wrote that she was "glad to see that this good old puritan custom is becoming popular throughout the nation." The previous year, she reported, twenty-one or twenty-two of the twenty-eight states observed Thanksgiving; seventeen did so on the same day. In 1862, she told readers that the number of states that celebrated the holiday in 1861, the first year of the Civil War, had grown to twenty-four plus three territories. All but two states—Massachusetts and Maine—celebrated the "annual Festival" on the last Thursday of November.

Hale's interest in creating a national Thanksgiving holiday went back to the time when she was still living in New England, and her early writings carry references to the holiday. She first wrote about Thanksgiving in 1827, in *Northwood: A Tale of New England,* devoting a chapter of the novel to describing a Thanksgiving that a visitor from England celebrates with a family in New Hampshire. She took up the topic again in *Traits of American Life,* a book of essays published in 1835. In a chapter titled "The Thanksgiving of the Heart," she wrote: "There is a deep moral influence in these periodical seasons of rejoicing in which a whole community participates."

The second edition of *Northwood,* published in 1852 and subtitled

Life North and South, expanded on the notion of Thanksgiving and called for it to become a national event:

> "Is Thanksgiving Day universally observed in America?" inquired Mr. Frankford [an Englishman on a visit to New England].
>
> "Not yet, but I trust it will become so. We have too few holidays. Thanksgiving, like the Fourth of July, should be considered a national festival, and observed by all our people."[6]

In *Godey's Lady's Book*, Hale helped consolidate support for her idea of a national Thanksgiving by publishing fiction and poems set around Thanksgiving Day. The holiday was depicted in highly sentimental terms. There were no dysfunctional families to be found in the short stories that graced the pages of *Godey's Lady's Book*. Rather, Thanksgiving Day was portrayed as a time of happy family reunions and bountiful tables. One such offering tells the fictional story of a wartime Thanksgiving, when a mother who has just sat down to dinner is surprised by the arrival of the son she believed had been killed in battle.

Hale promoted her campaign, too, by publishing recipes for traditional Thanksgiving dishes such as roast turkey and pumpkin pie. *Godey's Lady's Book* printed a recommended menu for Thanksgiving dinner that included New England classics as well as sweet potato pudding, a Southern standard. Hale's hope for a national Thanksgiving wasn't based on a desire to see Americans feast on the same foods on the same day, but she was shrewd enough to realize that the culinary appeal of Thanksgiving was another selling point for her vision of a shared celebration.

Meanwhile, Hale conducted a letter-writing campaign to lobby for a common national Thanksgiving. She wrote hundreds, perhaps thousands of letters to presidents, governors, congressmen, and other influential Americans across the country, soliciting their support for her project. She received little response.

President Zachary Taylor's reaction was typical. In 1849, he wrote an unknown correspondent (probably not Hale) who had suggested that the president appoint a day of national thanksgiving. "I have long thought it proper," Taylor replied, "to leave the subject of a thanksgiving proclamation where custom has so long consigned it—in the hands of the Governors of the several states."[7]

Despite the presidential rebuffs, Hale might have been indirectly responsible for what is said to have been the first Thanksgiving in the White House. Her campaign may have caught the attention of another Sarah—First Lady Sarah Polk, wife of the eleventh president, James Polk. Mrs. Polk acted as her husband's private secretary. There is no known correspondence between Hale and Polk, but if the president had received a letter asking him to declare a national Thanksgiving, his wife would have read it.

During his presidency, 1845–1848, Polk issued no Thanksgiving proclamations—perhaps in deference to his political mentor and fellow Tennessean, Andrew Jackson, who had expressed the view that the president's executive powers did not extend to naming a national Thanksgiving holiday. It was, however, a legal holiday in the District of Columbia during the years Polk was in office, having been so designated each year by the mayor. Polk's diary entries for Thanksgiving Day 1846, 1847, and 1848 mention that government offices were closed for the day. In his entry for 1847, the president wrote that he and his wife had attended church in the morning—another indication that he observed Thanksgiving. None of the entries mentions dinner.

That said, a Washington newspaper, reporting on Thanksgiving Day 1845, noted that the Polks had entertained some friends at dinner. Was this a Thanksgiving dinner? Or was it just one of many social events that the Polks hosted at the White House? According to John Holtzapple, director of the President James K. Polk House and Museum in Columbia, Tennessee, "If Sarah Polk hosted the first Thanksgiving dinner in the White House, her husband didn't recognize the importance of the occasion!"[8]

The number of states that celebrated Thanksgiving continued to mount. In 1847, Arkansas and Mississippi both proclaimed state Thanksgiving days, albeit on different dates. California had its first Thanksgiving Day in 1849, even before it was a state; the military governor named a day in a proclamation issued in both English and Spanish. Sam Houston, president of the Republic of Texas, named a Thanksgiving Day in 1842; Governor George T. White named the state of Texas's first Thanksgiving in 1848.

An exception to the Thanksgiving trend was Virginia, where two governors in the 1850s did not want any part of Thanksgiving, which had gained a reputation as a Yankee abolitionist holiday. In 1853, Governor Joseph Johnson, citing Thomas Jefferson's belief in the strict separation of church and state, declined to name a Thanksgiving Day. In doing so he won the support of pro-slavery Virginians, who objected to Thanksgiving's association with the abolitionist cause, as expressed by Protestant clergy who used the occasion of Thanksgiving Day to preach sermons against slavery.

Governor Johnson's successor, Henry Wise, a slaveholder, spoke bluntly in his reply to a letter from Hale in 1856 asking him to name a Thanksgiving Day. "The governor of Virginia is not authorized by her laws to call upon the people to bow to authority in heaven," he thundered. "This is no infidel or anti-Christian sentiment, but one founded on a zealous sense of preserving the Church pure from the State, and the State free from the Church."

Wise railed against churches that "profess to be Christian" and castigated the "thousand of pulpits" where ministers were preaching "Christian politics," which is to say inveighing against slavery. He told Hale he would not sign on to "this theatrical national claptrap of Thanksgiving," which was aiding the antislavery movement.[9]

The theme of Thanksgiving as having a "deep moral influence" on the national character—to use Hale's words—would recur again and again in her editorials for *Godey's Lady's Book*, especially as the country moved toward civil war. Hale believed a national celebration of Thanksgiving Day would help preserve the union. "Such social rejoicings," she editorialized in 1857, "tend greatly to expand the generous feelings of our nature, and strengthen the bond of union that finds us brothers and sisters in that true sympathy of American patriotism."[10]

Two years later, in 1859, she again stressed her belief in the unifying effect of a national Thanksgiving. "If every State should join in union thanksgiving on the 24th of this month," she wrote, "would it not be a renewed pledge of love and loyalty to the Constitution of the United States, which guarantees peace, prosperity, progress, and perpetuity to our great Republic?"[11]

Even as war loomed in 1860, Hale renewed her argument, writing that a national Thanksgiving could help keep together the divided country. "This year the *last Thursday in November* falls on the 29th," she wrote. "If all the States and Territories hold their Thanksgiving on that day, there will be a complete moral and social reunion of the *people* of America in 1860. Would not this be a good omen for the perpetual political union of the States?"[12]

Hale's Thanksgiving editorials were the closest she got in print to expressing a political view. Godey barred any discussion of politics in his *Lady's Book*—he apparently considered it an unsuitable subject for women—and he fired a writer at another of his magazines for writing that slavery ought to be abolished. If Hale wanted to share her views about slavery or the coming war with the readers of *Godey's Lady's Book*, she had to do so without direct reference to current events. Godey's no-politics editorial policy continued during the war. A reader who picked up a copy of *Godey's Lady's Book* between the years 1861 and 1865 would have had a hard time realizing that the Civil War was going on.

On September 28, 1863, Hale wrote a letter marked "Private" to President Lincoln. "Permit me," she began, "...to request a few minutes of your precious time." The subject she wished to lay out before the president, she wrote, "is to have the day of our annual Thanksgiving made a National and fixed Union Festival." The editor asked the president to "issue his proclamation for a Day of National Thanksgiving" for the last Thursday of November. She also implored him to "appeal to the Governors of all the States" to do the same. "Thus the great Union Festival of America would be established."

Hale mentioned that she had already written to Secretary of State William Seward, whom she knew when he was governor of New York, and asked him to "confer with President Lincoln" on the subject. The result, as we know, was Lincoln's decision to declare a national day of thanksgiving. Seward, who had issued Thanksgiving proclamations during his years in Albany, drafted Lincoln's proclamation.

The following year, 1864, Lincoln issued another Thanksgiving proclamation, again naming the last Thursday of November as the date of the holiday. According to the Washington *Evening Star*, Thanksgiving Day 1864 "was very generally observed." People "set themselves to a hearty observation of the day, not forgetting to pay due attention to that estimable feature of the occasion, the *Thanksgiving Dinner*, which sent up its appetizing odor throughout the length and breadth of the city."[13] Lincoln was dead by the time the next autumn came round.

As for Hale, she retired from *Godey's Lady's Book* in December 1877 after forty years at the helm. Her mind remained strong and she never stopped writing, working at her desk in her room at her daughter's house in Philadelphia. Shortly before she died on April 30, 1879, at the age of 90, *Godey's Lady's Book* published Hale's reflections on her campaign for a national Thanksgiving.[14]

"This idea was very near to my heart," she wrote, "for I believe that this celebration would be a bond of union throughout our country, as well as a source of happiness in the homes of the people." She went on to express her satisfaction that every president since Lincoln "has regularly issued his proclamation fixing a day for a National Thanksgiving."

But there remained a snag. While the overwhelming majority of governors went along with the date the president named for Thanksgiving and issued their own state proclamations conforming to the date the president had appointed, they were under no obligation to do so. The president's proclamation did not have the force of law outside the District of Columbia and U.S. territories. That would require an act of Congress.

In her late-in-life reflections on her Thanksgiving campaign, the lady editor—indefatigable to the end—made it clear that her work was not finished. Her dream of a national Thanksgiving "needs now only the Sanction of Congress to make it permanent," she wrote.[15] For that, the country would have to wait until 1941.

CHAPTER SIX

The Turkey Bowl

Thanksgiving Day is no longer a solemn festival to God for mercies given.
It is a holiday granted by the state and the nation to see a game of football.
— The New York Herald

Lincoln's successor, President Andrew Johnson, followed the lead of his predecessor by proclaiming a day of national thanksgiving in 1865. He did so the following year too, and by 1867 he was confident enough to assert in his proclamation that the idea of a national Thanksgiving Day had been accepted throughout the country. This "recent custom," Johnson wrote, "may now be regarded as established on national consent and approval."

The date of the annual national Thanksgiving was also becoming established. With the exception of 1865, when Johnson chose Thursday, December 1, the rest of the Thanksgivings during his presidency were held on the last Thursday of November. In 1869, Ulysses S. Grant declared the third Thursday of November as Thanksgiving, but that was his sole deviation from the last-Thursday pattern. By the end of his presidency, the last Thursday in November had become the accepted date for the holiday. The national Thanksgiving tradition was now launched. The president would issue a proclamation naming a day for Thanksgiving. The individual governors would concur and issue their own proclamations naming the same date. All Americans gave thanks on the same day.

Presidents and governors can proclaim holidays, but it is up to the people to embrace them and make them their own. There were still pockets of resistance to Thanksgiving in the South, where not every state saw fit to celebrate it during the postwar Reconstruction years. Governors sometimes changed the date of Thanksgiving in an apparent slap in the face to the president, or they called special Thanksgivings to further their own political aims. Texas was one of the last holdouts. Oran Milo Roberts, governor from 1879 to 1883, refused to issue a Thanksgiving proclamation, declaring, "It's a damn Yankee institution anyway."[1] But most Americans—including, eventually, Southerners—came to welcome their new national holiday with enthusiasm. Thanksgiving may have started out as a "damn Yankee" holiday, but it wasn't long before all Americans claimed it as their own.

The second half of the nineteenth century and the early twentieth century was a golden age for Thanksgiving, when the holiday was idealized in art, literature, and the popular press. One of the most recognizable Thanksgiving images was—and still is—George Henry Durrie's painting *Home to Thanksgiving*, published as a lithograph by Currier &

Ives. *Home to Thanksgiving* has graced countless calendars and greeting cards since it first appeared in 1867.

The scene is a New England farm on a bright wintry day. A well-dressed young family has just stepped out of an elegant horse-drawn sleigh. An elderly couple is greeting them on the front porch. Grandma, wearing an apron—has she just come from basting the turkey?—stands in the open doorway. She is holding a toddler, who, the viewer imagines, has jumped out of the sleigh and run into her arms. Grandpa is shaking hands with the young man, presumably his son or son-in-law, and with the other hand he is reaching out to the young woman. Snow, which was often featured in depictions of Thanksgiving, was more commonplace in late November in New England than it is today. A cooling period known as the Little Ice Age brought severe weather to New England and northern Europe from about 1300 to the middle of the nineteenth century.

Home to Thanksgiving is an idyllic scene that projects a feeling of nostalgia, family warmth, and happy contentment. The scene is unmistakably the New England countryside, but it nevertheless projects a sense of Thanksgiving's universal appeal. Take away the snow, it seems to say, and similar scenes are playing out all over the country on Thanksgiving Day.

As she campaigned for a national Thanksgiving in the 1840s and 1850s, Sarah Josepha Hale anticipated that the holiday would bind together the northern and southern halves of the fracturing nation.

After the Civil War, Thanksgiving helped bring the country together in another way. It became a potent symbol of national unity amid the growing ethnic, religious, and racial diversity of the American people. This attitude is best exemplified by Thomas Nast's 1869 cartoon "Uncle Sam's Thanksgiving Dinner."

Nast was a popular illustrator and political cartoonist who first rose to fame for his powerful sketches of slavery and Civil War battle-fields. Lincoln called him the "best recruiting sergeant" for the Union army because his work had inspired so many to join up. He worked for *Harper's Weekly*, the pre-eminent political and literary journal of the era, with a large national circulation.

Nast was an immigrant, having arrived in America from Germany when he was six years old, and "Uncle Sam's Thanksgiving Dinner" reflected what he saw as the immigrant's passionate affection for his new country and commitment to its democratic values. "Uncle Sam's Thanksgiving Dinner" is a utopian vision of a welcoming and inclusive country.

At the head of the table stands Uncle Sam, who is carving a turkey. Around the table are seated Americans representing an array of races and religions, identified in many cases by their national dress. Among the guests are an African-American family, a Native American, a Chinese man with a long queue, an Irish American couple, a Spanish woman wearing a mantilla and holding a fan, a bearded Muslim with a fez on his head. Nast presents the people in this portrait respectfully, not as caricatures. His message is that every American has an equal right to sit at the Thanksgiving table.

Opposite Uncle Sam, at the other end of the table, is "Columbia," the female figure Nast often used to represent America's democratic values. Her positioning between a black man and a Chinese man gives visual expression to the ideals of equality and inclusiveness, and to the artist's support of civil rights for minorities.

These themes are reinforced in other aspects of the cartoon. On the wall behind Uncle Sam is a painting of Castle Garden under a banner that says "Welcome." Castle Garden, in lower Manhattan, was the main processing center for immigrants entering the United States before Ellis Island opened in 1892. The table's centerpiece bears the words "Self Government" and "Universal Suffrage." In the two bottom corners of the cartoon, Nast wrote: "Come One Come All" and "Free and Equal."

The cartoon carries an overt political message. A sash reading "15th Amendment" hangs above a portrait of Ulysses S. Grant, who was then the president of the United States. Nast was endorsing ratification of the new constitutional amendment to guarantee the voting rights of all Americans regardless of race. Just as all Americans have a right to sit at the Thanksgiving table, Nast was saying, they also have a right to share in the full benefits and responsibilities of citizenship.[2]

After the Civil War, Americans continued to give thanks at morning worship services on Thanksgiving Day—in Jewish synagogues, Mormon temples, and Protestant churches. There was a notable exception to this practice: Catholic churches, which refused to celebrate the Puritan holy day. "The Catholic church had been willing to hold services on the civilly mandated days of thanksgiving proclaimed for special victories and for peace after the Civil War," explains Diana Karter Appelbaum, "but the idea of saying mass for an annual holiday proclaimed by civil authority—not to mention one that had been started by Protestants—was unacceptable." Individual Catholic priests might acknowledge Thanksgiving at regular weekday Mass, but the church did not encourage the practice until 1884, when Catholic bishops, meeting in Baltimore, "commended the holiday to their fellow churchmen."[3]

The second half of the nineteenth century, however, was also a period during which Thanksgiving Day churchgoing among Protestants diminished, with churches banding together to hold union services that would attract enough worshippers to fill the pews. Expressions of gratitude were still a dominant feature of the day, but fewer people made time to give thanks in their houses of worship on the day itself. The religious activities of the day gave way to the secular ones—family gatherings, turkey dinners, and, to an increasing extent, recreations. Which brings us to football.

A few days before Thanksgiving 1900, a newspaper in Virginia published the following lighthearted item. It appeared under the headline "Origin of Thanksgiving Day":

"We ought to do something to make ourselves solid with posterity," remarked one of the Pilgrim Fathers.

"That's so," replied his companion. "How would it be to inaugurate a national holiday that will be a convenient time for football games?"[4]

This squib—published on the newspaper's front page, no less—indicates that by the time the nineteenth century was ending, America's love affair with Thanksgiving football was well entrenched.

Football and Thanksgiving have gone hand in hand since the 1870s and probably earlier. No less an authority than the father of American football, Walter Camp, traced the beginnings of the sport back to Thanksgiving Day festivities in early New England. "In America," he wrote, "the first football was a peculiar Thanksgiving Day custom of kicking an inflated pig's bladder about the 'yard' of New England farmhouses, to the great merriment of the younger members of the household and the occasional discomfiture of the elders."[5]

There is a hint—the barest of hints, to be sure—that the game that millions of Americans now watch on the fourth Thursday of November may even have been a feature of the First Thanksgiving in Plymouth in 1621. In his description of that event, Pilgrim Edward Winslow tells us that "amongst other Recreations we exercised our Arms." Winslow's choice of the word "Recreations" is tantalizing. It is a broad enough category to call up images of men running after a ball on a beautiful autumn day.

In Plymouth in the 1620s, amusements were forbidden on religious days of thanksgiving, as on Sundays, and in any case the industrious Pilgrims did not hold with idleness on any day of the week. But the harvest feast that has come to be known as the First Thanksgiving was not a religious occasion, and Governor Bradford apparently allowed the colonists to pass the time playing games. We know from Bradford's journal that the Strangers, as the non-Puritan colonists were called, played pitching the bar, stool-ball, and "such-like sports" on Christmas Day in 1621. Pitching the bar is a log-throwing or pole-throwing competition. Stool-ball is an early form of cricket in which a stool is used as a wicket.

The phrase "such-like sports" raises the possibility of football. The settlers of New England brought kicking-the-ball games with them from England, and Melvin Smith, author of a book on the history of American football, believes that the Pilgrims probably played one of those games.[6] Moreover, a kicking-the-ball game similar to soccer was popular with the Wampanoag, who played it on the beach with a deerskin ball stuffed with deer hair.[7] All of which is to say that the Pilgrims and the Native Americans might have enjoyed an early version of football at the First Thanksgiving.

Fast forward to the nineteenth century. In the post–Civil War industrial age, there was little time during an ordinary workweek for leisure pursuits. Workers spent twelve hours a day on the job, six days a week. There were no paid vacations and only four legal holidays: Washington's Birthday, Independence Day, Christmas, and Thanksgiving. It is no wonder that Thanksgiving became a time for leisure activities. It was one of the few days of the year that a family—or, more typically, the men of the family—could spare time for amusements. In many parts of the country, the late-autumn weather provided a good opportunity for outdoor pursuits, including football.

Thanksgiving Day football games are almost as old as the national holiday itself. The first intercollegiate football game took place in 1869—Princeton vs. Rutgers in New Brunswick, New Jersey—and Thanksgiving Day football games began a few years later. On November 30, 1873, Princeton and Yale faced off in Hoboken, New Jersey, in a Thanksgiving Day championship game. It was a success, and the game moved to New York City a few years later.

The Yale-Princeton Thanksgiving Day game in New York quickly became immensely popular, with attendance catapulting from five thousand spectators in 1880 to forty thousand in the 1890s. The game was not just an athletic contest. It was a major social event in which all levels of New York society—old and young, male and female, rich and poor—took part. In the words of Richard Harding Davis, writing in *Harper's Weekly* about the 1893 game, it didn't matter whether New Yorkers could tell "a touchdown from a three-base hit" or knew whether "Yale is a city, State, or club." They knew that "the Yales" and "the Princetons" were going to fight it out in New York, and they wanted to join in the fun even if they couldn't afford to buy a ticket to the game. Yes, the Princeton-Yale Thanksgiving was a spectacle, he concluded, but it was "still the greatest sporting event . . . this country has to show."[8]

As Thanksgiving Day approached, New Yorkers divided into two rival camps and "surrendered" themselves to the students and their game. "No one who does not live in New York can understand how completely [the game] colors and lays its hold upon that city," Davis wrote, "how it upsets and overturns its thoroughfares, and disturbs its rapid routine of existence, and very few even of those who do live in New York can explain just why this is so; they can only accept the fact."[9]

Football mania took hold of the city. On the day itself, churches moved the time of their Thanksgiving services up an hour to accommodate game-goers and fans; pastors didn't want to risk preaching their Thanksgiving Day sermons to empty pews. God and Mammon genuflected to the all-powerful King Football.

Early on Thanksgiving morning, throngs of New Yorkers would begin their pedestrian parade on Broadway, a kind of autumnal variation on the famous Easter Parade up Fifth Avenue in the spring. The paraders wore tokens of the team they supported: rosettes of Yale blue in their buttonholes or ribbons of Princeton orange and black affixed to their coats. Shops were shuttered for the holiday, but their windows were festooned with decorations in the colors of the shopkeeper's favorite team and photographs of the collegiate football stars. One haberdasher, a New Haven fan, displayed blue handkerchiefs in the breast pockets of the manikins in his store's show window.[10]

At ten o'clock, a procession of horse-drawn carriages, omnibuses, and other vehicles—all decorated in the college colors—began to line up at appointed spots at the lower end of Fifth Avenue. Passengers carried aboard lunch baskets of food and drink and sat down to a kind of nineteenth-century tailgate party. As the caravan began its slow four-mile journey uptown to Manhattan Field in the Polo Grounds in Harlem, it passed sidewalks lined three or four deep with well-wishers shouting "rifle-like" cheers for Yale and "hissing sky-rocket" yells for Princeton, as Davis described it. Houses and apartment buildings along the route to the playing field flew the requisite colors. The wealthy hung huge silk banners displaying gigantic Y's or P's outside their mansions, while the poor waved strips of colored cloth out their apartment windows. "It is like a circus procession, many miles long," said Davis.[11] *Harper's* paid Davis the unheard-of sum of five hundred dollars for his article.

Not everyone approved of this new tradition of Thanksgiving Day football. Even Davis, who had described the festivities with apparent delight, believed that New Yorkers' obsession with football obscured the significance of the day. As recently as ten years earlier, Thanksgiving "was an event of moment and meaning," he wrote. Now, the holiday is centered on "twenty-two very dirty and very earnest young men who are trying to force a leather ball over a whitewashed line."[12] The *New York Herald* took a similar antifootball theme, lamenting that "No longer is the day one of thanksgiving to the Giver of all good. The kicker now is king and the people bow down to him."[13]

By 1893, the faculties of Yale and Princeton also came to disapprove of the Thanksgiving Day football game in New York City. This was an age when educators believed they had a responsibility to guide the moral development of the students in their care as well as their intellectual advancement. The professors objected to the hoopla over the game, which they thought distracted students from their studies, and they were appalled at students' excessive behavior during the postgame revelries, which inevitably provoked drunken brawls that ended with Princetonians and Yalies being hauled off to jail. The press covered the postgame excesses with as much relish as they covered the Thanksgiving Day game itself, and the alcohol-fueled escapades they reported did not reflect well on the young collegians or the schools they attended. The college authorities decreed that future champion-ship games would be played on campus, where they could keep a better eye on the collegians and crack down on any shenanigans.

The Princeton-Yale game in New York was a catalyst for the creation of a popular audience for Thanksgiving football. In 1893, one hun-dred twenty thousand athletes played in five thousand Thanksgiv-ing games across the country, demonstrating an enthusiasm for the sport that stretched far beyond the Ivy League.[14] It was the Num-ber One athletic event of the season at numerous colleges. Notable Thanksgiving Day rivalries that began around that time include the University of Michigan vs. the University of Chicago, Howard Uni-versity vs. Lincoln University, and Stanford vs. the University of Cal-ifornia, Berkeley, a.k.a. "the Big Game."

The Big Game of 1900, played in San Francisco, became known as the Thanksgiving Day Disaster. With insufficient stadium seats available for the popular game, hundreds of fans clambered onto the rickety roof of a nearby factory, where they had a good view of the football field. The roof collapsed. Twenty-three people died, and many more were injured or maimed. Most of the victims were boys and young men from the neighborhood. The Thanksgiving Day Di-saster was—and still is—the worst accident at a sporting event in the United States.

Thanksgiving football also caught on at high schools and local athletic clubs. Teams scheduled their seasons around Thanksgiving, playing end-of-season championships on the holiday. The longest continuing high school rivalry features two of the country's oldest public high schools: Boston Latin, founded in 1635, and Boston English, founded in 1821. The two schools have played football every Thanksgiving Day since 1887. West of the Mississippi, the longest-running Thanksgiving Day contest pits two St. Louis–area high schools against each other. The Webster Groves Statesmen started playing the Kirkwood Pioneers on Thanksgiving Day in 1907.

Thanksgiving football is still going strong. There are about seventy-five high school rivalries dating back more than a hundred years, and dozens more are approaching their centennials. For high schools, Thanksgiving Day football games are community-building events, encouraging school spirit and deepening local pride. The tradition of watching a local football game can be a unifying force, in keeping with the inclusive spirit of the holiday. The author of a book about a long-running high school Thanksgiving game on Staten Island explains it well: "For one day a year...that corner of New York City had something in common with all those small towns in the South or the Midwest where the game pulled people together, and gave them an opportunity to feel like part of something bigger than themselves."[15]

By the time professional football leagues arose around the turn of the twentieth century, Thanksgiving football was a well-established tradition. For the pros, hosting a Thanksgiving game was a no-brainer. They figured that if colleges and high schools could attract crowds on Turkey Day, so could they. The New York Pro Football League, a predecessor of the National Football League, began scheduling its championship game for Thanksgiving. The Ohio League, another ancestor of the NFL, held its most important games on the holiday. The inaugural NFL season in 1920 featured six Thanksgiving Day games.[16]

In 1925, the first NFL superstar was born at Wrigley Field on Thanksgiving Day, when the Chicago Bears introduced their newest player, nicknamed the Galloping Ghost. Thirty-six thousand fans turned out to see Harold "Red" Grange, who had played his farewell game at the University of Illinois ten days earlier. The standing-room-only crowd was the largest in pro football at the time.[17]

The pro team most associated with Thanksgiving is the Detroit Lions, which have played on Thanksgiving Day for as long as they have been the Detroit Lions. The team started out in 1930 as the Spartans of Portsmouth, Ohio, a steel town on the Ohio River. In 1934, a Detroit radio station owner, George A. Richards, bought the Spartans, moved them to Michigan, and changed their name. The Lions drew lousy crowds in the first few weeks of the season, in part because the sports pages were more interested in covering the Detroit Tigers baseball club than in writing about the new football team. Richards decided he needed to do something to make a splash; he wanted a gimmick to get the attention of sports reporters and, he hoped, sell more tickets. He hit upon the idea of scheduling a Thanksgiving Day game against the Chicago Bears, who were the reigning champions. The publicity stunt worked. Tickets to the game sold out weeks before Thanksgiving, and fans were turned away at the gate. The Lions have played every Thanksgiving Day since 1934, aside from a break during World War II.

There is a similar story about the Dallas Cowboys. In 1966, the NFL wanted to schedule a second Thanksgiving Day game, and the Texas general manager, Tex Schramm, jumped at the chance to gain some publicity. The Cowboys were a young team—just six years old at the time—and Schramm hoped the Thanksgiving game would bring them national attention. He was right. Their game against the Cleveland Browns attracted a record crowd.

Today, the NFL holds three Thanksgiving Day games, two in the afternoon and one in the evening. The Lions and the Cowboys are holiday fixtures, and—unfair as it may seem to the other NFL teams—they always get to play at home on Thanksgiving. The third game was introduced in 2006, with no fixed teams.

Football may reign supreme, but it isn't the only sport associated with the holiday. Thanksgiving is one of the biggest workout days of the year, according to the *Wall Street Journal*. Cycling, rowing, running, and pumping iron are all popular holiday activities.[18] Thanksgiving is the biggest day of the year for running races. About eight hundred thousand people ran in Thanksgiving Day races in 2012, 2013, and 2014, according to Athlinks, an aggregator of athletic-event data. "Turkey Trots," as Thanksgiving Day races are often called, aren't new. Buffalo has been hosting a Turkey Trot since 1896, and the organizers say it is the oldest annual public footrace in the country. About ten thousand participants have taken part in recent years—some dressed up as Pilgrims, Indians, pumpkins, or turkeys. Seattle has a marathon called the Wattle Waddle. In Phoenix, there is a thirty-eight-mile Turkey Day Ride for cyclists.

Of course, most Americans still get their biggest workout on Turkey Day by pushing away from the table after dinner and walking to the TV to tune into the game. In 2015, the three Thanksgiving football games attracted 25.4 million viewers (Philadelphia Eagles at Detroit Lions), 32.5 million viewers (Carolina Panthers at Dallas Cowboys), and 27.8 million viewers (Chicago Bears at Green Bay Packers). Football is still the king of Thanksgiving sports.

As Thanksgiving football fever swept the nation at the end of the nineteenth century, it provoked a backlash from those who thought the emphasis on the sport detracted from the more important religious and familial aspects of the holiday. The meaning of Thanksgiving was hotly discussed from pulpits, in the newspapers, and around the dinner tables of ordinary Americans. Was Thanksgiving football a pernicious influence? Was its popularity intruding on family get-togethers and obscuring the religious obligation to give thanks to God and remember the less fortunate?

The *Chicago Tribune* entered the fray in 1896 when it published several pages of commentary about the nature of the holiday on the

Sunday before Thanksgiving. The lead story, which took up a full page, examined how the city's poor, sick, and imprisoned would spend Thanksgiving and raised the question of whether there would be too much football and too little thanksgiving on the coming holiday. It asked "where the greater happiness is to be derived—from the spectacle of athletic sports on the one hand or from that of ministering to those to whom those sports are forbidden on the other."[19]

The newspaper's Thanksgiving spread included essays by seven prominent Chicagoans who were asked to weigh in on the meaning of the holiday. They addressed the appropriate balance to be struck between God, football, and family.[20]

One clergyman warned of the encroachment of athletics on a day that properly belonged to home and family. Another clergyman disagreed, saying there was nothing wrong with a "family walk or spin on a wheel, the merry outdoor game, or even [a] more exciting football contest." He recommended dividing the day into three parts: church in the morning, football or other outdoor amusements in the afternoon, and family in the evening.

The president of Northwestern University was in favor of football and "amusements of the right kind"—no definition given—so long as they didn't conflict with church services. The dean of the Kent School of Law concurred, arguing that it was not a sacrilege that the day should be celebrated with football. "There is nothing irreligious or irreverent in athletics," he wrote. "A sound mind in a sound body is doubtless the greatest of all temporal blessings."

It fell to a local rabbi—an obvious football fan—to provide the most eloquent response on the proper role of football on Thanksgiving Day: "A good God will delight in a joyful, manly people and accept the shout of victory won in manly contest as a thanksgiving offering," he said. The rabbi drew upon the wisdom of the Old Testament Book of Ecclesiastes when he wrote: "There is a time for everything: a time to pray and a time to play."

CHAPTER SEVEN

Happy Franksgiving

I would prefer to trust Abraham Lincoln's judgment than Franklin D. Roosevelt's.
I would like to see Thanksgiving celebrated on the last Thursday in November.
— W. C. Adams, President, National-American Grocers Association

O n August 14, 1939, while vacationing at his boyhood summer home on Campobello Island, off the coast of New Brunswick, President Franklin Delano Roosevelt called an informal news conference. The president dropped a bombshell: He announced that he had decided to move Thanksgiving Day forward by a week. Rather than take place on its traditional date, the last Thursday of November, the annual holiday would instead be celebrated a week earlier.

The country was in the midst of the Great Depression, and the president's stated reason was economic. There were five Thursdays in November that year, which meant that Thanksgiving Day, if celebrated on the last Thursday, would fall on the 30th of the month. That left just twenty shopping days till Christmas. Moving the holiday up to November 23 would allow shoppers more time to make their purchases and—so the president's dubious theory went—spend more money, thus giving the economy a lift. Most Americans would have been happy to comply with the president's encouragement to spend more, if they had had the money. But they didn't, and the early Thanksgiving was just another example of the New Deal's ill-considered campaign to bring the country out of the Depression by persuading people to spend their way to prosperity.

At the Campobello Island press conference, Roosevelt said that businessmen had been pressing him to move Thanksgiving forward ever since he took office in 1933. The change in date would be permanent, he added. The president then offered a little tutorial on the history of the holiday. Thanksgiving was not a national holiday, he explained, meaning that it was not set by federal law. According to custom, it was up to the president to select the date every year.

It wasn't until 1863, when President Lincoln directed that Thanksgiving be celebrated on the last Thursday in November, that this date became generally accepted nationwide, Roosevelt explained. To make sure that reporters got his point, he added that there was nothing sacred about the date. The president then decamped for a sail in the Bay of Fundy on the cruiser *Tuscaloosa*, where he hosted a tea for a contingent of his neighbors at Campobello.[1]

Nothing sacred? Roosevelt might as well have commanded that roast beef henceforth replace turkey as the star of the holiday meal, or that cranberries be barred from the Thanksgiving table. The president badly misread public opinion. His announcement was front-page news the next day, and the public outcry was swift and vociferous.

Immediate disapproval was voiced from Plymouth, Massachu-setts. James Fraser, chairman of the selectmen of the town—that is, the mayor—said he "heartily disapproved" of Roosevelt's plan. "We here in Plymouth consider the day sacred," he said, contradicting the president. "Plymouth and Thanksgiving are almost synonymous and merchants or no merchants I can't see any reason for changing it."[2] He announced that he would put the matter before the Plymouth board of selectmen at their next meeting. A few days later, the pas-tor of Plymouth's Church of the Pilgrimage assailed the president's move as a "calloused attack on a religious tradition" and lamented that "the sacred has given way to the secular forces of life."[3]

There was also instant condemnation from the nation's college football coaches. The United Press news service, reporting from Campobello, noted mildly that coaches would find the date change "a considerable headache."[4] The Associated Press was less subtle about the coaches' likely reaction. The Roosevelt plan, it predict-ed, would "kick up more clamor than a hot halfback running the wrong way."[5]

By 1939, Thanksgiving football had become a national tradition. For many Americans, watching a bunch of young men toss a pigskin around on a field was as much a part of the holiday weekend as eat-ing turkey. Many colleges ended their football seasons with Thanks-giving Day games, and millions of fans looked forward to watching football on the holiday, a habit that, in some cases, dated back to the nineteenth century.

There was also the issue of the collegiate calendar. According to the rules of several college football conferences, the last game of the season had to be played by Thanksgiving weekend, thereby raising the question of how the schools could rearrange their schedules so that the final game of the season could be played a week earlier than planned. College deans complained, too, about the disruptions the new date would cause to academic schedules, but the press was more interested in reporting what the coaches had to say.

The 1939 fall football schedules had already been long established and printed by the time of Roosevelt's mid-August announcement. In a letter to the White House, the assistant to the chancellor of New York University explained his school's dilemma: "As you probably know," Philip Badger wrote the president, "it has become necessary to frame football schedules three to five years in advance, and for both 1939 and 1940 we had arranged to play our annual football game with Fordham on Thanksgiving Day, with the belief that such day would fall upon the [last] Thursday in November."

Badger framed his complaint politely: "Please understand that all of us interested in the administration of intercollegiate athletics realize that there are considerations and problems before the country for solution which are far more important than the schedule problems of intercollegiate athletics," he wrote. "However, some of us are confronted with the problem of readjusting the date of any football contest affected by the President's proposal."[6]

Joseph Labrum, athletic director of the University of Pennsylvania in Philadelphia, was also upset. He told the Associated Press that his school had printed up sixty-five thousand pieces of mail advertising the November 30 game between Penn and Cornell. Moreover, he said, changing the date "would spoil a forty-year tradition."[7]

Far from the Ivy League, in Arkansas, the coach of Little Ouachita College, when asked about Roosevelt's move, expressed himself more colorfully than the Philadelphian: "We'll vote the Republican ticket if he interferes with our football," the Southerner threatened. Arkansas was a firmly Democratic state, or as one sportswriter put it, this sacrilege came from a state "where Republicans are practically museum specimens."[8]

Meanwhile, politicians were tapping public opinion and issuing statements of their own. Alf M. Landon, the Republican presidential nominee who had lost to FDR in 1936, knew a political opening when he saw one. He was quick to condemn the date change—and not afraid to use over-the-top language. The president, he said, announced his decision to change the date "to an unprepared country with the omnipotence of a Hitler." He continued: "The president's sudden attempt to change Thanksgiving Day is another illustration of the confusion which his impulsiveness has caused so frequently during his administration."[9]

Since Thanksgiving was not a holiday established by federal statute, the president's annual proclamation of the date had the force of law only in the District of Columbia and United States territories, including Hawaii and Alaska. In most of the forty-eight states it was left to the governor to determine the date of the holiday, but the governors had almost always followed the president's cue. A few states had passed legislation mandating that Thanksgiving be marked on the date set by the president, but in most states, governors issued pro forma ratifications of the date the president proclaimed.

Not this year. Roosevelt's switch turned the date of Thanksgiving Day 1939 into a political hot potato. Now politicians in every state had to read public opinion, examine the local business climate, consider political loyalties, and then decide which date to endorse as the official Thanksgiving. Do they stick with tradition and celebrate the holiday on November 30, or follow FDR's lead and change the date to November 23?

The forty-eight states were nearly evenly divided on the question. Twenty-three decided to stick with November 30, while twenty-two adopted FDR's date of November 23. The remaining three—Texas, Mississippi, and Colorado—said they would celebrate on both days.

States opting for the "New Deal Thanksgiving" on November 23 were: California, Delaware, Georgia, Illinois, Indiana, Louisiana, Maryland, Michigan, Missouri, Montana, New Jersey, New York, North Dakota, Ohio, Oregon, Pennsylvania, South Carolina, Utah, Virginia, Washington, West Virginia, and Wyoming.

The lineup of traditionalists opting to celebrate on November 30 was: Alabama, Arizona, Arkansas, Connecticut, Florida, Idaho, Iowa, Kansas, Kentucky, Maine, Massachusetts, Minnesota, Nebraska, Nevada, New Hampshire, New Mexico, North Carolina, Oklahoma, Rhode Island, South Dakota, Tennessee, Vermont, and Wisconsin.

It wasn't long before people started referring to November 30 as the "Republican Thanksgiving" and November 23 as the "Democratic

Thanksgiving" or even "Franksgiving." But opposition to the new date did not strictly follow party lines.

The six New England states, all led by Republican governors, were unified in opposing the date change. The governor of Massachusetts, Leverett Saltonstall, when asked for reaction to FDR's announcement, said he "would hesitate a long time before" he would make a change and called the proposal "more upsetting than advantageous." He added, "Think also how tremendously disturbing it would be to school and college vacation schedules which have already been made up for this year."[10] Senator Styles Bridges of New Hampshire wasn't so polite. He sarcastically suggested that Roosevelt break another tradition: "Has the president given any thought to abolishing winter?" he inquired.[11]

Out west, the Republican governor of Wyoming, Nels Smith, also condemned the date change, saying, "I do not approve of any change in the long-established date for Thanksgiving, which will only create confusion." He took the opportunity to make a political point by conceding, "This is one program the president has demanded which is not imposing any additional tax on the taxpayers."[12] The Democratic governors of Iowa, Oklahoma, North Carolina, and Arizona also announced their immediate disapproval.

Most Democratic governors, however, spoke out in support of FDR. Governor Culbert Olson of California said the president's plan "meets with my approval." Governor Herbert O'Conor said that "Maryland recognizes the right of [the] nation's Chief Executive to select [a] suitable date," and that the state's residents are so "appreciative of [the] manifold blessings they enjoy that they offer thanksgiving every day."[13]

In parts of the Midwest, no one—Democrat or Republican—seemed to care much. "At the moment I don't see that advancing the Thanksgiving date would make a lot of difference out here in Nebraska," volunteered Governor R. L. Cochran, a Democrat. In Michigan, the Republican governor, Luren Dickinson, agreed. "I don't see that it makes much difference," he said, adding, "Personally, I shall be just as thankful on November 23 as on November 30." Payne Ratner of Kansas, also a Republican, echoed these sentiments: "It doesn't make much difference to me whichever day we observe Thanksgiving," he said. "I prefer to interest myself in seeing to it that whichever day it is we'll have something for which all of us can lift our praise to Almighty God in real thankfulness."[14]

Texas, living up to its reputation for doing things big, had a compromise solution: Celebrate both holidays. Governor W. Lee "Pappy" O'Daniel, a Democrat, said he would issue a proclamation naming both November 23 and November 30 as Thanksgiving days. Colorado followed suit and declared that it also would celebrate twice.

Politicians aside, public sentiment ran heavily against Roosevelt's plan. Ten days after the president's announcement, the Gallup organization published the results of a national poll: only 38 percent of Americans surveyed said they favored the date change, while the remaining 62 percent disapproved. George Gallup summed up his findings: "The survey shows that a majority of Americans—and particularly Republicans—are in favor of letting the nation's turkeys live a week longer."[15]

This wasn't the first time in American history that the public had objected to a date set by the central authorities for Thanksgiving. The national rebellion against Franksgiving recalled an episode in the 1680s when New Englanders rebelled against a Thanksgiving date set by the royal governor appointed by the British Crown. It was an early example of colonists' resentment of English tyranny and it presaged the anger that erupted into the Revolutionary War in the next century.

Sir Edmund Andros, royal governor of the Dominion of New England, usually carried out his charge from Boston, but he was on a visit to Connecticut in the autumn of 1687 when the ministers of churches in Massachusetts met and agreed to name November 17 as a day of thanksgiving. Andros returned to Boston on November 16 and immediately invalidated the ministers' proclamation, declaring that only the royal governor had the authority to appoint a day of thanksgiving. He named December 1 as Thanksgiving Day for all of New England. Most New Englanders reluctantly went along with the governor's date. The exception was the people of Rhode Island, who refused to allow an Englishman to tell them when to worship. In defiance of the governor's proclamation, which set the day apart for prayer, they went to work on December 1 and refused to attend religious services.

Andros, the representative of the Catholic King James II, eventually got his comeuppance. The Glorious Revolution in England the following year resulted in elevating Protestant sovereigns to the throne. New Englanders threw Andros into jail and proclaimed days of thanksgiving for the ascension of William and Mary.

In 1939, the White House received thousands of letters opposing President Roosevelt's decision to advance the date of Thanksgiving.

From South Dakota came a letter from Robert S. Benson and Clarabelle Voight, who signed themselves as "representatives of the northwest":

> ...this country is not entirely money-minded, we need a certain amount of idealism and sentiment to keep up the morale of our people, and you would even take that from us. After all we want to make this country better for our posterity, and you must remember we are not running a Russia or communistic government.
>
> Between your ideas of running for a third term, and your changing dates of century old holidays, we believe you have practically lost your popularity and the good will of the people of the Northwest.[16]

Eleanor Lucy Blydenburgh, a student at the Pratt Institute in Brooklyn, also disagreed with the president. In FDR's home state of New York, Thanksgiving would be celebrated on November 23, but Miss Blydenburgh's home state of Connecticut had designated November 30 as Thanksgiving. She wrote the president to complain that she would be unable to celebrate the holiday with her family:

Your recent decision to change the date of our Thanksgiving Day has just taken effect here at Pratt Institute. Our directors announced that our school vacation would begin on the twenty-third of November and last until the twenty-sixth because New York, being your home state, is abiding by your decision. However, where I come from, Connecticut, they'll be observing it on the thirtieth of November as usual. Really, this situation makes my heart ache because I love our Thanksgiving Holidays as much if not a bit more than our Christmas Holidays.

Oh, I've missed one other Thanksgiving at home with my parents because I was away at college and too far away to get home to celebrate with them and I didn't like being away at that time either but I see its [*sic*] going to happen again.

I would really like to know just why you did change the date, my curiosity has been aroused. You probably won't see or hear of this letter because you are so busy however, it's been nice writing you about the situation.[17]

One F. P. Archer Sr., tongue firmly in cheek, dispatched a telegram to Roosevelt from Miami:

Mr. President: Please inform those who disagree with your advance Thanksgiving date that every day is Thanksgiving in Florida. We who love healthful sunshine, bounteous harvests of fruits and vegetables and the clean, cool breezes from the Gulf Stream never cease thanking Almighty God for these daily blessings.[18]

Roosevelt had made his decision to advance the date of Thanksgiving in part on advice from the secretary of commerce, Harry Hopkins, who was in turn influenced by Lew Hahn, general manager of the Retail Dry Goods Association. Hahn had warned Hopkins that the late Thanksgiving, November 30, might have an adverse effect on the sale of holiday goods.

Other retailers shared Hahn's view. In 1933, another year with a late Thanksgiving, the chairman of the Downtown Association of Los Angeles had written the president urging the date change:

> It is an established fact that Christmas buying begins vigorously every year in the retail stores the day following Thanksgiving and that the Thanksgiving to Christmas period is the busiest retail period of the whole year.

> The Downtown Association of Los Angeles feels that Abraham Lincoln's Proclamation of 1864 setting aside a day for Thanksgiving to be the 4th or last Thursday in November of each year can be carried out to the letter by designating in your Thanksgiving Proclamation this year, November 23rd, the fourth Thursday in November as the day of Thanksgiving.

> You will appreciate the importance that an additional week incorporated in this great holiday season will have upon the distribution activities of the entire United States and the added impetus that will be given thereby to the efforts of the administration and the N.R.A. [National Recovery Administration] to increase employment and purchasing power.

The Downtown Association of Los Angeles respectfully requests your consideration of this practical suggestion, believing that your approval would have the deep appreciation of the merchants of the entire country.[19]

Not all retailers shared this view. Also in 1933, Cleveland's Richman Brothers Company, which described itself as America's largest clothing manufacturer, sent the president a telegram expressing its protest against "the selfish attempt of a small group of stores to change the date of Thanksgiving Day." Quite aside from the "hallowed traditional reason," the clothiers' telegram read, "we believe the proposed change would hurt more merchants than it would help." The Richman Brothers' reason? "It would shorten the season and curtail the fall business of clothes and all seasonable goods for the benefit of novelty and small gift items."[20]

In 1939, a similar view was expressed by Charles Arnold of the Arnold Men's Shop in Brooklyn, New York, who wrote the president that he would like to "give you the view point of the small merchant in regard to your change of the Thanksgiving date." The small storekeeper, Arnold said, "would prefer leaving Thanksgiving Day where it belongs. If the large department stores are over-crowded during the shorter shopping period before Christmas, the overflow will come, naturally, to the neighborhood store." He closed by asking Roosevelt to "Kindly reconsider and oblige thousands of small retail storekeepers throughout this country."[21]

Other businesspeople who were opposed to Roosevelt's date

change included producers of the star attraction of Thanksgiving dinner: turkey growers. The president of the National Poultry, Butter and Egg Association sent a skeptical telegram to the White House:

> Poultry of all kinds, and particularly turkeys, is very heavily marketed prior to and for the Thanksgiving holiday. Your contemplated change will be injurious to many producers and disrupt marketing plans of processors and distributors.[22]

People in the calendar industry, which prints its products a year or two in advance, were apoplectic. Typical was a letter from John Taylor of the Budget Press in Salem, Ohio. He wrote the president:

> Your change for Thanksgiving naturally makes all 1939 calendars obsolete, as well as all 1940 calendars, although it is not too late to change the preliminary work for 1941.
>
> I am afraid your change for Thanksgiving is going to cause the calendar manufacturers untold grief. If very many customers demand 1940 calendars to correspond with your proclamation, hundreds of thousands of dollars will be lost by the calendar companies, and in many instances it will result in bankruptcy.
>
> You will realize, I am sure, that if you had purchased calendars last January for delivery this coming December, to be distributed January 1940, you would want those calendars to show the correct date for Thanksgiving, and you would expect the manufacturer to furnish them—Presidential Proclamation notwithstanding. Due to

the fact that 90% of the calendars will be showing Thanksgiving on the usual date for 1940, your Presidential Proclamation should be rescinded; and if it is necessary to change Thanksgiving it should not be changed until 1941. Otherwise, it is going to be difficult for calendar manufacturers to get their customers to use the calendars already printed.[23]

For the next two years, Roosevelt continued to move up the date of Thanksgiving—to November 21 in 1940 and to November 20 in 1941. More states resigned themselves to celebrating early. By 1941, however, the facts turned against Roosevelt.

By then, retailers had had two years of experience with the early Thanksgiving, and data were available on the 1939 and 1940 Christmas shopping seasons. In mid-March 1941, the *Wall Street Journal* reported the results of a survey conducted by the New York City Department of Commerce at the behest of Mayor Fiorello La Guardia. The *Journal*'s headline put it succinctly: "Early Thanksgiving Not Worth Extra Turkey or Doll." Of the stores surveyed in the Big Apple, 77 percent reported that the observance of a different date in adjoining states hurt their business. Only 37 percent favored the early date, while the rest either opposed it or didn't care one way or another.[24]

In Washington, the Commerce Department reached the same conclusion. The early Thanksgiving resulted in no boost to retail sales. A majority of stores, it found, reported that the date shift had little or no effect on sales. And so, on May 20, the president called a press conference at the White House and announced that he was changing Thanksgiving Day back to its traditional date. The earlier date had been an "experiment," he said, and the experiment failed. It was too late to move the 1941 holiday back, he said, since businesses and calendar makers had already acted on his commitment to the early date. But in 1942, Thanksgiving would revert to the last Thursday of the month.[25]

"This is the last year we shall be called upon to celebrate a New Deal Thanksgiving," a *Washington Post* columnist exulted. "In 1942 and after, by grace of Presidential rectification of error, Thanksgiving will be [on] the old date, not dictated by trade but inspired by sentiment." The columnist dubbed Roosevelt's announcement "the first time any New Deal experiment was voluntarily abandoned."[26]

The Roosevelts marked Thanksgiving Day 1941 quietly. Due to the growing tensions with Japan, they stayed in Washington rather than travel to Warm Springs, Georgia, where they usually celebrated the holiday with the patients and staff of the polio rehabilitation center the president had founded there. Their only guests were their son James and his wife. "Franksgiving" that year fell on November 20.

A week later, the Roosevelts were able to get away from Washington in time to attend a rescheduled Thanksgiving dinner in Warm Springs on Saturday, November 29. The president carved the turkeys and the polio patients prepared their usual program of skits and songs. After the program, Roosevelt delivered impromptu remarks.

He began with a lighthearted reference to his failed campaign to move up the date of Thanksgiving. Two or three years ago, he said, "I discovered I was particularly fond of turkey," and so "we started two Thanksgivings." He went on to talk about how he had enjoyed listening to football games on the radio that afternoon, especially the contest between West Point and Annapolis.

But then his tone turned somber. He reminded the audience that while Americans could be thankful that year for a peace that had lasted since World War I had ended in 1918, much of the world was again at war. "We need to be thoroughly thankful that these years of peace were given to us," he said. "It may be that next Thanksgiving these boys of the Military Academy and of the Naval Academy"—the ones who had been playing football that afternoon—"will be actually fighting for the defense of these American institutions of ours."[27]

It would be four years before a president of the United States and the American people would observe the holiday by giving thanks for being a nation at peace. On Sunday, November 30, the day after his Thanksgiving dinner in Warm Springs, FDR was urgently recalled to Washington. One week later, the Japanese bombed Pearl Harbor and the United States was at war.

On December 26, 1941, the day after Christmas, Roosevelt signed a joint resolution passed by Congress making Thanksgiving an official national holiday and mandating that it be celebrated on the fourth Thursday in November.

CHAPTER EIGHT

Day of Mourning

The first Thanksgiving was all right. It started to fall apart after that.
— Bill Wasden, Native American

N ative Americans mostly celebrate Thanksgiving in the same way that other Americans do, with the three F's: family, feasting, football. It is a day for sharing time with relatives, eating the traditional meal, and watching sports on TV. But for some Native Americans, the central aspect of the day—giving thanks—can be tricky.

As Americans, Indians value the holiday as a day set apart to pause and count their blessings. As Native Americans, they recognize that while the First Thanksgiving represented a moment of amity between indigenous people and newcomers from the Old World, it also heralded a tragic period for their people and culture. For that reason, Thanksgiving can also be a time to reflect on the history of Native Americans' encounters with the European colonists and to remember their ancestors who died in conflicts with the newcomers.

There is a small group of extremists in the Native American community who adhere to a radical view of Thanksgiving Day. Their

viewpoint was summed up by the comedian and political commen-
tator Jon Stewart in the quip: "I celebrated Thanksgiving in an old-
fashioned way. I invited everyone in my neighborhood to my house,
we had an enormous feast, and then I killed them and took their
land." Anti-Thanksgiving activists reject the holiday, viewing it as the
beginning of the end for the indigenous peoples of North America.
As one activist put it, "We're here because some white man didn't kill
our ancestors."[1]

A more nuanced view is expressed by the chief of the Mashpee
Wampanoag nation on Cape Cod, Cedric Cromwell, who explains
the complex nature of the holiday for many Native Americans.
In a Thanksgiving Day message to his community, Chief Cromwell wrote: "The Thanksgiving holiday is a complicated day for our
people. We are forever entwined with the American Thanksgiving
myth, however inaccurate it may be." Without offering judgments,
Cromwell lists the choices that Native Americans face as they decide
how to mark the holiday: "Some of our people choose to observe this
day as a Day of Mourning. Some choose to celebrate in a thoroughly
American way. Many choose a different path, spending the day with
family and friends, but acknowledging our unique history and connection to this day."[2]

An irony here is that two of the heroes who dominate the story of
the First Thanksgiving are Indian: Massasoit, the great chieftain of
the Wampanoag Confederation; and Squanto, the Patuxet Indian
who befriended the Pilgrims. Massasoit and Squanto made the First
Thanksgiving possible. Without them, the tiny band of Pilgrims who

had made it through the bitter winter of 1620–1621 would probably not have survived. Massasoit lay the groundwork for the peace that reigned on Thanksgiving Day and for most of the half century that followed. Squanto was responsible for the successful harvest that supplied the food the Pilgrims put on the Thanksgiving table.

Massasoit possessed keen diplomatic skills. He forged personal ties with Pilgrim leaders, including Edward Winslow, who, when Massasoit fell seriously ill in 1623, helped nurse him back to health. Winslow relates that upon his recovery, Massasoit told him that "the English are my friends and love me" and promised that "whilst I live I will never forget this kindness they have shown me."[3] Massasoit was true to his word. But after his death in 1661, the goodwill he had established gradually dissipated, culminating in 1675 in the devastating King Philip's War, led by Massasoit's second son, Metacomet, or King Philip. The English victory in 1678 virtually ended traditional Indian tribal life in southern New England.

As for Squanto, the story of how he taught the Pilgrims to plant corn using fish as fertilizer and directed them to good fishing spots is told in many elementary schools. One of the gripes of Native Americans—and not just extremists—is that children don't learn about Squanto's tragic background, which includes being abducted by European traders and sold into slavery. Squanto's travails presaged the sorrows that would befall the indigenous people of North America after the arrival of the Europeans.

For years before the *Mayflower* landed at Plymouth, European trading ships had been visiting the area. Sometimes the traders kidnapped young Indian men to sell as slaves or put on display as human curiosities for Europeans who had never seen a "red" man.

Squanto was kidnapped twice. The first time (around 1605, by some accounts), he was taken to England, where he was treated well, learned English, and then was sent with an expedition back to his homeland in 1614. He was quickly abducted again, this time by an English trader who took a number of Indian men to Málaga, Spain, to sell into slavery. They were rescued by Franciscan friars and introduced to Christianity. The friars apparently nurtured Squanto's dream of one day returning home, and they helped him get to London, where eventually he was able to earn one-way passage on a ship to New England in exchange for service as an interpreter. When he finally reached his home village in 1619, he found it deserted. Every member of his family and all of his friends had been wiped out by a disease, probably smallpox, that had been carried to the New World by Europeans.

The next year, 1620, the Pilgrims chose the site of Squanto's former village as the location for the settlement they named Plymouth. The following spring, they were amazed when an Indian man speaking fluent English appeared seemingly out of nowhere and offered them his assistance. He became their indispensable man—interpreter, teacher, counselor, go-between. When Squanto died in November 1622, he bequeathed his meager belongings to his English "friends"—to use Governor Bradford's word—"as remembrances of his love, of whom they had a great loss."[4] Squanto's friendship with the Pilgrims changed everything, making it possible for them to stay alive and thrive.

For some Native Americans, though, the Thanksgiving story, including the lifesaving contributions of Massasoit and Squanto, are overshadowed by the history of Indian death and displacement that followed. In this line of thinking, the traditional Thanksgiving story is a half-truth and deserves to be seen in the context of the coming tragedies and the poverty and racism with which many Native Americans struggle today. These naysayers use the day to call public attention to Native American history and to current government policies that affect Indians. Some also celebrate Thanksgiving in the traditional way; others don't want anything to do with it.

Dennis Zotigh works as a cultural affairs specialist at the Smithsonian's National Museum of the American Indian. He is a Kiowa, San Juan Pueblo, and Santee Dakota Indian from Oklahoma. For several Thanksgivings, the museum posted on its website a popular column written by Zotigh in 2011. It is titled "Do American Indians Celebrate Thanksgiving?"[5]

In his column, Zotigh doesn't mention how he and his family spend Thanksgiving, but he makes it clear that he finds the holiday troubling. Many Native Americans, especially in New England, he writes, see Thanksgiving as a reminder of the attempted genocide of their people. He estimates that three hundred thousand Indians died in the violence that engulfed New England after the half century of relative peace that followed the Pilgrims' arrival at Plymouth.

He also objects to the idea that the Thanksgiving feast of 1621—

or any other thanksgiving celebrated by the Pilgrims—was the "first." The Pilgrims did not introduce the concept to the New World, he notes. The New England Indian tribes had been celebrating harvest feasts of thanksgiving long before the *Mayflower* carried the Pilgrims to Plymouth. "To the original people of this continent," he writes, "each day is a day of thanksgiving to the Creator." A number of Indian leaders stress this point—that in Indian culture, every day is a thanksgiving day. Cromwell, the Mashpee Wampanoag chief, has written that "Blessings occur every day as the Creator casts his light upon us."

Zotigh reserves his most strenuous criticism, though, for how Thanksgiving is taught in elementary schools. Presenting the First Thanksgiving as primarily a happy time "trivializes our shared history and teaches a half-truth," he writes. He objects, also, to Thanksgiving re-enactments that expose children to false images of Indian culture that stick with the children for the rest of their lives and, he says, perpetuate historical inaccuracies.

He gives the example of the wearing of feathers, which carries solemn significance in Indian culture. The Thanksgiving costumes that kids dress up in bear no resemblance to what the Wampanoag wore in that era, and in Zotigh's view they make a mockery of Wampanoag traditions. (It is worth noting that accuracy and respect are often lacking in familiar portrayals of Pilgrims. Those ubiquitous buckles on the Pilgrim hats that children wear are not authentic, for example. And it would be a rare public school that dared to include in its Thanksgiving pageant a scene of Pilgrims holding Bibles or praying.)

Judging from the avalanche of comments that Zotigh's column

sparked online, many Native Americans share his dismay about how Native Americans are portrayed in elementary school lessons on Thanksgiving—portrayals they view as inaccurate and disrespectful, with lasting consequences for how Americans perceive Indian culture.

Zotigh goes on to express the belief that children in elementary school are too young to know the truth about Native American history, which is too violent and too complex for them to comprehend. In his view, teachers need to "share Thanksgiving facts in all American schools sometime before high school graduation."

That is exactly what some high schools and colleges say they are doing. Unfortunately, facts can get lost when seventeenth-century American history is viewed from the perspective of twenty-first-century mores—which is to say, through the prisms of race, gender, ethnicity, and identity politics. Often, the results are not pretty.

Consider the following email that the Student Government Association of Barnard College in New York City sent out to every student. It reached students' in-boxes shortly before Columbia University, of which Barnard is a part, closed for Thanksgiving vacation in 2013. The email read in full:

> Happy Turkey Week. Thanksgiving is complicated. We urge you not to forget that this holiday commemorates genocide and American imperialism. But, enjoy the week off and make it into something meaningful.

Thanksgiving commemorates "genocide" and American "imperialism"—but go ahead and live it up. Something is missing here. Whatever happened to the idea of gratitude? Or reuniting with family? Or tolerance, diversity, and inclusion? Are students at one of America's top institutions of higher education really so ignorant about these aspects of Americans' favorite holiday?

The answer, regrettably, may be yes.

Children still learn the basics of the holiday in elementary and middle school, though not always accurately, as Zotigh correctly pointed out. If students happen to study Thanksgiving in high school—and many don't—the risk is that their teachers will use the holiday as a jumping-off point to rail against colonialism, cultural imperialism, and the displacement and murder of Native Americans by European settlers. The online Zinn Education Project, which provides lesson plans and supplementary material to accompany Howard Zinn's leftist bestseller, *A People's History of the United States*, offers one example of the kind of material that some young Americans are being taught.

Among the materials the Zinn Education Project provides for classroom use is an essay on the history of Thanksgiving. It is full of inaccuracies and bizarre interpretations.[6] To wit:

★ The holiday is used by government leaders as a political tool. Lincoln, the essay says, initiated the holiday "to rouse northern patriotism for a war that was not going well." But in fact, the tide of the Civil War had turned toward the North in 1863, when Lincoln issued his first proclamation of a national Thanksgiving.

★ The essayist can't resist a swipe at George W. Bush, who paid a surprise Thanksgiving Day visit to American soldiers in Iraq in 2003. The purpose of the visit was not to support American troops in a faraway land, students are told, but "to rally the public behind an invasion based on lies."

★ Governor William Bradford's *On Plymouth Plantation*, one of the masterpieces of American literature, is a "fable" and an "early example of 'Euro think.'"

★ As for Thanksgiving Day itself, students are informed that the holiday celebrates "aggression and enslavement."

Zinn's *A People's History of the United States* has sold more than two million copies and is assigned reading in many high schools and colleges.

A touchstone of revisionist teaching on the Thanksgiving holiday is the Pequot War of 1637, at whose conclusion the victorious settlers of New England held a day of thanksgiving. Anti-Thanksgiving activists like to present this as the "true" history of the holiday. They point in particular to the event known as the Mystic Massacre, when English settlers and their Narragansett and Mohegan allies wiped out a Pequot village, brutally killing several hundred men, women, and children. The Zinn Education Project essay references the massacre as one of the primary influences on our Thanksgiving Day.

So, too, a prominent Indian-rights activist angrily informed me that the day of thanksgiving held after the massacre was the bloody progenitor of the holiday that Americans mark today. Type the words "Thanksgiving massacre" into a search engine and dozens of articles show up about the Mystic Massacre, many of them making the same or similar claims. When a young relative and I got talking about Thanksgiving at a family party, a shadow fell across his face and he asked, citing his history teacher, "Didn't the Pilgrims celebrate Thanksgivings after they murdered Indians?" This young relative attended one of the top-rated public high schools in the country.

The true history of the Mystic Massacre is more complex. It was a grisly episode in the bloody Pequot War, which lasted nearly a year, pitting the Pequot Indians against English settlers in Connecticut and their Mohegan and Narragansett allies. There was brutality on both sides, with Pequots attacking English settlements, scalping farmers as they walked to their plots outside village walls, and kidnapping children to hold for ransom. The English returned the favor by killing and enslaving Pequots. In May 1637, in the wake of an attack that killed nine settlers, the English set fire to the Pequot village in what is now Mystic, Connecticut. As the village went up in flames, they shot Pequots who tried to escape, while the Narragansett and Mohegans, waiting in the woods, clubbed to death any who managed to elude the English guns.[7]

The Mystic Massacre was a turning point in the war. The Pequots were defeated that summer, and the English gave thanks for their victory. The early American historian Benjamin Trumbull recounted how a day of public thanksgiving was named, and "in all the churches of New-England, devout and animated praises were addressed to Him, who giveth his people the victory, and causeth them to dwell safely." He called the victory a "happy event" that "gave great joy to the colonies."[8]

To reject our present-day Thanksgiving because of the Pequot War and the English victory thanksgiving is absurd, akin to rejecting

George Washington's pre-eminent place in the founding of the United States because he owned slaves. No one ought to feel guilty for celebrating Thanksgiving, but the dominant message in some American classrooms is that guilt is appropriate.

A University of Texas professor has argued for Thanksgiving to be replaced with a national Day of Atonement and collective fasting to "acknowledge the genocide of indigenous people that is central to the creation of the United States."[9] Thanksgiving, writes Robert Jensen, is a "white supremacist holiday." The professor berates as hypocrites his fellow liberals who celebrate the holiday even though they share his view that Thanksgiving is based on a "mythology" that "amounts to a kind of holocaust denial." He urges readers to boycott Thanksgiving gatherings and, when possible, participate in a public event that "resists" Thanksgiving. This radical interpretation of the holiday is not widely shared, but neither is it an unusual point of view in the academy.

The most extreme example of Native Americans rejecting Thanksgiving is found in Plymouth. Every Thanksgiving Day since 1970, a group of Native Americans gather there to mark what they call a National Day of Mourning. Thanksgiving, they say, is a reminder of "the genocide of millions of Native people, the theft of Native lands, and the relentless assault on Native culture." While most of their countrymen feast, these nonconformists fast.

The idea for a day of mourning in memory of Indians who have died since the arrival of the Europeans dates back to 1836. William Apess, a Methodist minister who was part Pequot, called for Indians to observe a solemn remembrance on Forefathers Day, the anniversary of the Pilgrims' arrival in Plymouth. Apess was among the first public advocates of equal rights for Indians. In his sermons and books he excoriated non-Native Americans for what he saw as their savage mistreatment of Indians. He was a powerful public speaker, and as an itinerant minister he carried his message to many congregations in New England. He was also one of the first prominent Native American writers, author of the autobiography *A Son of the Forest*, and the influential *Eulogy on King Philip*, the Wampanoag leader and son of Massasoit who led the losing Indian forces in the bloody King Philip's War. After Philip's death, as Apess relates in unsettling detail, his body was quartered, his hands were cut off, and his head was set on a stake in Plymouth, where it stayed on public display for years.

"Let the children of the Pilgrims blush," Apess wrote in *Eulogy on King Philip*, "while the son of the forest drops a tear and groans over the fate of his murdered and departed fathers." He called Forefathers Day and the Fourth of July "days of mourning and not of joy," and he urged "every man of color [to] wrap himself in mourning" on those patriotic holidays. "Let them rather fast and pray to the great Spirit, the Indian's god, who deals out mercy to his red children, not destruction."

The first modern-day National Day of Mourning took place on Thanksgiving Day 1970. That year was the three hundred fiftieth anniversary of the landing of the Pilgrims in Plymouth, and Frank James, a Wampanoag, had been invited by the organizers of the local festivities to give a speech at a celebratory dinner. When the organizers learned that James intended to use the occasion not to focus on the friendship between the Pilgrims and his Wampanoag ancestors but, rather, to mourn the near-extinction of his tribe and the wider tragedy of the continent's Native American people, they demanded that he revise his speech. He refused and withdrew from the anniversary program.

There are many poignant passages in James's undelivered speech, which he signed with his Native name, Wamsutta. The tone is mournful rather than angry or combative. Read at a distance of nearly forty years, in an age marked by ruder rhetoric, his speech seems mildly phrased—more a song of sorrow for the Indian people than an indictment of the Pilgrims. He wrote: "We, the Wampanoag, welcomed you, the white man, with open arms, little knowing that it was the beginning of the end; that before fifty years were to pass, the Wampanoag would no longer be a free people."[10] He did not mention Thanksgiving.

James's exclusion from the anniversary proceedings sparked anger among some in the Native American community, to the extent that James and a group calling themselves the United American Indians of New England (UAINE) decided to hold a protest on Thanksgiving Day. That was 1970. Since then, Indians and non-Native supporters gather at noon every Thanksgiving Day near the statue of Massasoit at the top of Cole's Hill, overlooking Plymouth Harbor. The rally on Cole's Hill is followed by a march through Plymouth's historic downtown district, and then a potluck meal in the social hall of a local church, where those who have been fasting break their fast. Frank James died in 2001. His son, Moonanum James, and

Mahtowin Munro, a Lakota Dakota, lead the annual protest today. Over the years, Day of Mourning participants have staged a few attention-getting stunts. They have dumped sand and seaweed on Plymouth Rock, boarded the replica of the *Mayflower* in the harbor, and draped Ku Klux Klan sheets on the statue of William Bradford. In 1997, participants tangled with police, who said they needed a permit for their rally—though that had never been a requirement in the past—and arrested several marchers for disorderly conduct when they refused to disperse.

The case was resolved in 1998 with both the police and protestors cleared of wrongdoing. The town agreed to pay UAINE's legal fees along with $100,000 toward educational programs on Native American history. It also agreed to put up two plaques. One, placed in Plymouth's Post Office Square, honors Metacomet, a.k.a. King Philip. The other plaque offers what UAINE calls an alternative view of Thanksgiving, and it stands in a prominent spot on Cole's Hill. It characterizes Thanksgiving as "a day of remembrance and spiritual connection as well as a protest of the racism and oppression which Native Americans continue to experience."

Activists on the other coast have been holding their own Thanksgiving alternative on the island of Alcatraz in San Francisco Bay since 1975. Originally called Un-Thanksgiving Day, the event began as a commemoration of the occupation of the abandoned island by activists in the Red Power movement from November 1969 to June 1971. The Alcatraz occupation marked the unofficial start of the modern-day Indian rights movement.

Today the Thanksgiving alternative event is organized by the International Indian Treaty Council, an advocacy group for Indian rights that has consultative status at the United Nations. In the mid-2000s, the council rejected the name Un-Thanksgiving as too confrontational and replaced it with Indigenous People's Thanksgiving, which it viewed as a more appropriate characterization of the event. "We realized that the most important thing was to uplift our history and the history of our people since colonization," said Andrea Carmen, the Indian Treaty Council's executive director and a member of the Yaqui Indian nation. "We give thanks for our survival."[11]

Indigenous People's Thanksgiving gets under way before dawn on Pier 33 on San Francisco's waterfront, where participants line up in the dark to catch the first boat to Alcatraz at 4:45 a.m. Once on the island, the participants—typically several thousand people—gather in a massive circle around a sacred fire to welcome the dawn. There are drummers, dancers, speeches, and songs. It is a solemn spiritual event, said Carmen. "We have lots to be thankful for, and let's talk about that. Our ancestors kept our spiritual traditions, our culture, our history alive. We are thankful in spite of what happened to us. We continue to be a living, spiritual force in our homeland."

The gathering concludes by 9 a.m.—in time for participants to get home and put a turkey in the oven. Unlike the protestors at the much smaller National Day of Mourning in Plymouth, many of the participants in the Alcatraz event celebrate Thanksgiving Day with their families in the usual way. Carmen sees no contradiction in that. "We're an intercultural people," she says. It is natural that many Indians would want to mark the day with both of the traditions they value.

In a way, the Indigenous People's Thanksgiving is a throwback to the time when Americans went to church on Thanksgiving morning before heading home to dinner. So, too, the Native American Thanksgiving ceremonies on Alcatraz feed the soul; it is a time for remembering one's ancestors and reflecting on one's blessings. The rest of the day is devoted to family gatherings and an enormous feast. Carmen— who grows her own pumpkins for Thanksgiving pies—says it well: "I myself would not miss it."

CHAPTER NINE

Helping Hands

Let us freely give to the children of penury and want among us.
— The Washington Daily Intelligencer

Sarah Josepha Hale identified one of the enduring features of Thanksgiving as "generous beneficence to the poor."[1] This observation remains as true today as it was in 1870, when the editor of *Godey's Lady's Book* wrote it. At no time of the year is American generosity more evident than at Thanksgiving, when large numbers of Americans donate to charitable causes and volunteer their services to help the less fortunate.

This tradition of generosity dates back to early colonial days. The earliest recorded reference to charity toward the poor in connection with Thanksgiving is from December 22, 1636, when the town of Scituate in Massachusetts set aside a day of thanksgiving for the first time. Church documents record that religious services were held in the "Meetinghouse" from 8:30 in the morning until just past noon. The afternoon was spent in "making merry," with "the poorer sort being invited of the richer."[2]

At some point, it became customary for churches to take up collections for "the poorer sort" on Thanksgiving Day or in the weeks leading up to it, so that the donations could be distributed in time to help recipients arrange for a good dinner on the holiday and prepare for the coming winter. The opening paragraph of an article published in the *Connecticut Courant* on December 1, 1766 is illustrative. It was datelined Boston and described how Thanksgiving Day had been spent in that city:

> Yesterday was observed here as a Day of general Thanksgiving. On this Occasion large Collections were made in many or most of the Churches in Town for the Relief of the Poor and Indigent, to enable them the better to provide against the Inclemency of the approaching Season.[3]

In his travels around the United States in the 1830s, Alexis de Tocqueville famously observed that Americans were constantly forming voluntary associations for the purpose of mutual aid and support. The inspiration for many such organizations was concern for the poor, with special attention given to their plight on Thanksgiving Day. Some of these charitable organizations still operate. The Bowery Mission has been feeding and sheltering homeless New Yorkers since 1879. The Salvation Army has been helping the poor in America since its founding in Philadelphia in 1879. Goodwill got its start in Boston in 1902 and then spread nationwide.

Consider this letter to the editor of the *Hartford Daily Courant* from a woman at the local city mission, which was founded in the

1850s. The letter carried the headline "Thanksgiving and the Poor" and was published a week before the holiday in 1882. The writer made a public appeal for assistance in making sure that poor families in the community were able to experience what she called "a Thanksgiving day and spirit":

> Thanksgiving time is here again, and again, as for thirty years past, the City Mission wishes to do its part for the needy poor, that it may be a thankful time for them as for the more fortunate. And therefore we ask the public for support of money and food that will enable us to give to our poor families a Thanksgiving day and spirit; that fathers and mothers in our care may feel the warmth and strength of human sympathy and Christian helpfulness about them. We shall receive most gratefully whatever is given us for them: food, money, groceries, comforts for the old and sick, etc.
>
> We also ask for clothing, shoes, bedding &c., of which many are sorely in need. If the old shoes of children are brought to us they will be put to immediate use, for we see children every day who are staying from school because they have no shoes.
>
> The winter is close upon us and the poor need all the light and cheer of the holidays to carry them through, as do we all.
>
> Virginia T. Smith,
City Missionary[4]

The relationship between Thanksgiving and generosity was reinforced thousands of times in the popular press of the day—in news articles about how the poor marked the holiday and how kind individuals, religious institutions, and charitable organizations came to their aid; in commentaries praising do-gooders and exhorting readers to do their part; and in the publication of sermons by local clergy urging readers to lend assistance to their fellow citizens.

The fiction of the nineteenth and early twentieth centuries is replete with uplifting moral tales of charity toward the less fortunate on Thanksgiving Day. A short story published in *Godey's Lady's Book* in 1863 is typical of the genre. In this particular story, a neighbor delivers a Thanksgiving dinner to a mistreated child by the name of Roxy, who exclaims: "I never expected to eat a mouthful to-day; and here's a real Thanksgiving dinner for me! Chicken pie! cold ham! biscuit! cake! and I don't know what else!"[5]

A story published in the *Cambridge Chronicle* of Massachusetts a week before Thanksgiving 1888 provides another illustration. As the tale opens, a street urchin is daydreaming about the Thanksgiving feast he wishes he could eat when his reverie is interrupted by a disturbance nearby. A gunshot rings out, a man flees, and the boy gives chase. His identification of the criminal is helpful to the police, who express their thanks by giving him a dinner as fine "as a Vanderbilt need want."[6]

The master of the American short story, O. Henry, wrote a brilliant variation on this theme in his moving tale of "Two Thanksgiving Day Gentlemen."[7] Stuffy Pete is down-and-out and living on the streets of New York City. Every Thanksgiving afternoon for the past nine years, an elderly gentleman has met Stuffy Pete on a park bench in Union Square and treated him to a magnificent dinner at a nearby restaurant. This year, however, Stuffy Pete has already eaten dinner, courtesy of two rich old ladies who also have a Thanksgiving tradition of feeding the poor. When the old gentleman turns up as usual at his park bench, Stuffy Pete, seeing that the man's eyes were "bright with the giving-pleasure," doesn't have the heart to tell him he is not hungry. The duo go off to the restaurant, where the old gentleman watches happily as Stuffy Pete forces himself to eat another huge meal. After dinner, the men part. Now comes one of O. Henry's distinctive twisty endings. The old gentleman collapses and is taken to the hospital, where it turns out he hasn't eaten in three days. He had been saving his money so that he could give Stuffy Pete a grand dinner on Thanksgiving Day.

Americans are the world's most generous people. When it comes to charitable giving, they are twice as generous as the Canadians or the British and ten or twenty times as generous as the people of other developed countries such as France, Germany, and Japan. Annual charitable giving accounts for 2.1 percent of the American gross national product, compared with 1.2 percent in Canada, 0.8 percent in the United Kingdom, and a paltry 0.1 percent in Germany. No other country comes close to the United States in its philanthropic donations.[8]

In 2014, Americans donated $358.38 billion to charity. Of that sum, an astonishing 73 percent, or $258.51 billion, came from individual donors. Personal gifts from individual Americans account for four times as much, every year, as what foundations and corporations give away.

Americans have a long tradition of individual giving. Consider the following example from the Civil War. On Thanksgiving Day 1864, the second of the national Thanksgivings proclaimed by Lincoln, hundreds of small donations made it possible for five hundred wounded and sick soldiers at Armory Square Hospital in Washington, D.C., to enjoy a Thanksgiving dinner.

As reported in a local newspaper, the cost of the holiday meal for the soldiers and a regiment of veterans assigned to work as nurses or guards at the hospital was $390. The Wesley Chapel Sunday School contributed $100, a sum that would have been collected in small donations from congregants. The American Telegraph Company and Adams & Co. each gave $20, the Sanitary Commission donated $5, and a Mrs. Platt of Connecticut gave $15. The rest of the total was made up of far smaller individual gifts. Similar stories of Thanksgiving generosity played out at all the hospitals in Washington, as Americans reached into their pockets to make sure that wounded soldiers ate well on the holiday.[9]

As this story of Civil War philanthropy indicates, charitable giving in America is not limited to the wealthy. Throughout American history, people from all walks of life and wide degrees of means have given generously to charity. A significant portion of Americans' annual charitable giving—as high as one-half, according to one survey of nonprofits—is done during the "giving season," the period stretching from Thanksgiving to Christmas.

As in so many other matters, George Washington provided an example for Thanksgiving generosity. In conjunction with the issuance of his Thanksgiving proclamation in 1789 (as noted earlier), the first president made a donation of twenty-five dollars to the Presbyterian Church with instructions that it be used for the benefit of New York City's poor. In addition, on Thanksgiving Day he donated beer and hot meals to imprisoned debtors in New York. In his biography of Washington, Ron Chernow writes that "It was a rare instance in which [Washington] allowed his contribution to be made public, presumably because he thought it appropriate to set an example for the rest of the country."[10] The man who was, as the saying goes, "first in war, first in peace, first in the hearts of his countrymen" was also a first-rate philanthropist.

The tradition of Thanksgiving generosity also takes the form of volunteer work. The ladies who hosted the holiday dinner for wounded soldiers at Washington's Armory Square Hospital in 1864 were not paid workers. They offered their services as cooks, servers, and companions. They decorated the dining hall, set the tables, cooked the meal, served the food, and assisted amputees who needed help walking to the dining hall or cutting their meat.

For many Americans today, helping a fellow American celebrate Thanksgiving is personal, sometimes intensely so. Volunteers sort food at local food banks, prepare and serve meals at soup kitchens, and deliver Thanksgiving dinners to shut-ins. Among the saddest images in American culture is that of a fellow citizen with nowhere to go on Thanksgiving, and volunteers often aim to extend a sense of family to people who find themselves alone on the holiday. Many community centers and churches strive to personalize their Thanksgiving dinners, eschewing buffet lines in favor of seating at tables with family-style service. A church in Seattle assigns members as table hosts, whose job it is to welcome guests, make them feel comfortable, and watch for indications that they might need extra help.[11] A common refrain is that the volunteers get more out of the experience than they give.

Such was the case for Patricia Yarberry Allen, a Manhattan physician who volunteered at her church on Thanksgiving Day 2015. She had donated her services in food kitchens before, but was always busy behind the scenes and did not interact with guests. This time, however, she joined an elderly man for lunch at one of the tables. Jim, who lived in the neighborhood, was eighty-seven years old and had no family members with whom to spend the holiday. She listened as Jim shared memories, especially of the dogs he had loved over the course of his life.

Allen likened her interaction with Jim to the story of Mary and Martha in the New Testament. In that story, Jesus pays a visit to the home of two sisters, Mary and Martha. Martha rushes off to prepare food for their guest, while Mary sits at Jesus' feet and listens to his teachings. When Martha asks Jesus to tell Mary to help her with the work, Jesus replies that Mary has made the better choice. Allen wrote of her Thanksgiving Day experience: "I understood spiritually how Mary had benefited from just being present, from witnessing and remembering the stories, even though Martha had done all the work."[12]

At the Community Soup Kitchen and Outreach Center in Morristown, New Jersey, as many as three hundred people gather each year for Thanksgiving dinner. The soup kitchen has been providing holiday meals to people in the community for more than a quarter of a century. Some are elderly, some are homeless, some are mentally ill, and some are families and individuals who have recently fallen on hard times. Volunteers from nearly three dozen church congregations staff the center.

In 2011, the Morristown Division of Health ruled that under New Jersey laws, the soup kitchen was a "retail establishment." Among other things, this designation brought with it a prohibition on volunteers donating food they had prepared at home. The food kitchen now had the additional expense of purchasing food instead of being able to rely on donations. But something more than money was lost. For volunteers, the regulation eliminated an important personal connection to the people they fed. Yes, they could write a check instead of baking a cake and delivering it to the food kitchen, but it wasn't the same. For those whom the food kitchen served, it meant no more home-baked desserts, no more homemade lasagna, and so forth. In the words of a columnist who wrote about the food kitchen's woes, it was now "more institutional cafeteria than Grandma's house."[13]

The Bureau of Labor Statistics calculates that sixty-three million Americans—which amounts to 26 percent of adults—volunteered time to a charitable cause in 2013. According to the BLS, the average amount of time given by volunteers was two hundred thirty-three hours per year, for a total of 8.1 billion hours. That is a low estimate, since volunteer activity by its nature often goes unrecorded. There are no breakout statistics of how much volunteer work is performed around Thanksgiving, but informal soundings indicate that it is substantial.

Thanksgiving is the busiest time of year for those who are in the business of combating hunger—a category that includes the army of volunteers at the Connecticut Food Bank. Four thousand Connecticuters donate their services at the food bank every year. Thousands more volunteer at the more than seven hundred community-based food programs throughout the state that the food bank provisions. The food bank estimates that it provides food for more than half a million meals a year. Similar scenarios play out at Thanksgiving time in every one of the fifty states.[14]

In the week before Thanksgiving, the Connecticut Food Bank's warehouse in Wallingford is bustling with activity. SUVs and vans line up in the parking lot early in the morning, waiting for their turn to back up to a loading dock and collect the crates of food they have pre-ordered for their soup kitchens and food pantries. Most of the vehicles belong to private citizens who are making a pickup run on behalf of the community or religious organization for which they volunteer. They have emptied out their trunks and back seats to make room for frozen turkeys, sacks of fresh yams, and boxes jammed with canned cranberry sauce, gravy, corn, and the other traditional fixings of Thanksgiving dinner.

Inside the vast warehouse—whose exterior is designed to resemble the ubiquitous red barns of the Connecticut countryside—things are humming. In the sortation room, a group of thirty volunteers from Prudential Annuities in the nearby town of Shelton has set up an assembly line to sort, box, and label frozen meat that has been donated by a local supermarket. It is a team-building exercise for the Prudential workers, as employees from various departments take part; an event planner, for example, works side by side with a sales manager and a product developer. Everyone is wearing blue and white T-shirts emblazoned with the company logo. For the Prudential workers, volunteering at the food bank can also be an eye-opening look at the challenges that poor people encounter in one of the richest states in the country. During the orientation session, a Prudential man who sounds like he is used to taking charge sputters with outrage when he learns that in order to qualify for food assistance from the state, a person has to submit a twenty-six-page application form and wait a month for approval. What if the applicant has a hard time reading or writing in English, he inquires. Or what if he is hungry *now* and can't wait for his application to be reviewed? The woman who is conducting the orientation session shrugs her shoulders. She has no answers for Mr. Take-Charge.

Over at the long corridor known in-house as Produce Alley, another source of Thanksgiving generosity is on display in the form of yams. A close examination of the traditional holiday side dish reveals that these yams—there is no way to put this politely—are uglier than the ones you are likely to encounter at your local supermarket.

They are too big, too small, or too misshapen for the retail market, which is why they ended up at the food bank. Yam growers in the South donated their rejects to a national feeding program that in turn shipped them off to food banks around the country. Similarly, apple growers in Connecticut have donated boxes of their fruit.

Just off Produce Alley is a storage area crammed with totes, which are large bins on wheels that the Connecticut Food Bank uses for food drives. The totes, holding up to one thousand pounds each, are placed at malls or outside stores to be available for donations from the public. These particular totes were used in a food drive sponsored by a local radio station at a nearby supermarket the previous evening. Deejays from the station took turns greeting customers in front of the store and encouraging them to donate frozen turkeys or packaged food that could be eaten at Thanksgiving dinners. The totes hadn't been unpacked or sorted yet, and you could see a mishmash of products: boxes of instant potatoes and stuffing mix, cans of cranberry sauce, cartons of apple juice. The supermarket chain sells prepacked boxes of Thanksgiving trimmings—ten items for ten dollars—and many shoppers have bought one or more such boxes to contribute to the tote. The box is labeled "GIVE THE TRIMMINGS OF A HOLIDAY MEAL TO THOSE IN NEED." The savvy supermarket chain was meeting a market demand with its "trimmings" box. Realizing that its customers wanted to purchase food for needy neighbors, it helped make that easier to accomplish.

Communities have come up with a variety of other ways to facilitate donations. In Middletown, as in other towns and cities around

Connecticut, churches coordinate food collections from their congregants. Each church is assigned a particular Thanksgiving item—
the Methodists might collect stuffing, the Catholics gravy, the Con-
gregationalists canned corn, and so on.

But it is the story of the birds that best illustrates the extent and
variety of Thanksgiving generosity. The birds, of course, are turkeys. The Connecticut Food Bank gives away twenty thousand
frozen turkeys at Thanksgiving time, and the staff begins lining up
donations in the summer. Some of the turkeys come from in-house
philanthropy programs at local businesses and nonprofits. The employees at Waterbury Hospital, for example, donate three hundred
birds. Subway has a program whereby employees at the more than
three hundred Subway locations in Connecticut can decline their
annual gift of a Thanksgiving turkey and give it instead to the Connecticut Food Bank. A local supermarket chain donates one thousand turkeys.

Food drives are another source of turkeys. At Thanksgiving time,
the food bank sends a refrigerator truck to the large food drives it
sponsors at supermarkets. Donations of frozen turkeys will be safely
transported in the truck back to the warehouse, where they will be
stored in the warehouse's freezer until it is time to give them away. A
refrigerator truck is also dispatched to the annual Fill the Bowl outreach program at the Yale Bowl in New Haven on a Saturday before
Thanksgiving. Donate a frozen turkey along with two nonperishable
items, and get two tickets to that afternoon's football game.

"Thanksgiving is all about the bountiful table," said Paul Shipman, an executive at the Connecticut Food Bank. The food bank's chief goal is to provide Thanksgiving dinners for people who might not otherwise be part of the celebration, "but we also want to provide an opportunity for people to help." Helping, too, is part of what Thanksgiving is about—and a way of giving thanks for what you have.

Sarah Josepha Hale hoped to see the celebration of the American Thanksgiving spread to the four corners of the world one day. That hasn't happened. Instead, two other days associated with the holiday have gone global: Black Friday and Giving Tuesday.

Retailers worldwide participate in Black Friday, which is almost as well known in Brazil and Bulgaria as it is in the United States—though if you asked a Brazilian or a Bulgarian what holiday preceded Black Friday, you would be met with blank stares. Outside the United States, Black Friday takes place outside the context of Thanksgiving.

In many countries, as in the United States, Black Friday is the unofficial start of the Christmas shopping season and a day when retailers offer great deals in stores and online. In the United States, stores open early on Black Friday, and some even open the night before, to the dismay of traditionalists who want to keep the Thanksgiving holiday free of commercial activity.

There are several fanciful explanations for how Black Friday got its name. One explanation—which is false—says it refers to slaveholders' practice in the South of taking their slaves to market on the day after Thanksgiving. Another explanation, also untrue, is that it derives from the fact that many retailers sell enough on that day to move their accounts from the "red" into the "black." A third theory, which may be true or partially so, is that it originated in the 1950s when so many workers called in sick on the day after Thanksgiving that an unknown wag coined the term "Black Friday" in allusion to the "Black Death" of the fourteenth century. Apparently, day-after-Thanksgiving-itis was as virulent as the bubonic plague.

A fourth theory—and one that makes a lot of sense—is that the name arose from a post-Thanksgiving traffic nightmare. According to Joseph P. Barrett, who was a police reporter for the now-defunct *Philadelphia Evening Bulletin*, weary traffic cops in the late 1950s or early 1960s invented the term to describe the congestion in downtown Philadelphia on the day after Thanksgiving. The city was flooded with suburban shoppers and out-of-town visitors arriving for Saturday's Army-Navy game. Barrett and a co-author appropriated the term from the traffic police for a page-one story on the terrible traffic conditions, and it stuck. "We used it year after year," Barrett wrote. "Then television picked it up."[15]

Black Friday gets a bad rap. A popular view is that Black Friday is the anti-Thanksgiving—that it is all about getting, not giving. After a day dedicated to the virtue of gratitude, Americans give in to a frenzy of consumerism and the vice of greed. Or so say Black Friday's detractors. But that isn't the full picture. In a free-market economy, getting and giving are connected. A strong economy—as reflected by strong sales on Black Friday—means that more Americans have jobs, higher incomes, and greater means to take care of themselves and extend generosity to the less fortunate.

Which brings us to Giving Tuesday, often known by its Twitter handle, #GivingTuesday. In contrast to Black Friday, Giving Tuesday is directly related to the spirit of Thanksgiving.

Giving Tuesday is the brainchild of the 92nd Street Y, a venerable Jewish community and cultural center on the Upper East Side of Manhattan. Inaugurated in 2012, Giving Tuesday's objective is to harness the power of social media to encourage individuals to give to the charities of their choice. The founders selected the Tuesday after Thanksgiving as the day for the annual campaign because of the link between gratitude and generosity.

The idea for Giving Tuesday began with Thanksgiving, according to Henry Timms, executive director of the 92nd Street Y and the principal force behind the creation of Giving Tuesday. "We talked about the holiday, and we saw that we, as Americans, had lost sight of the best and most meaningful things" about it, he said. Timms and his colleagues came up with the idea of adding a new day to the calendar of the extended holiday. "It's a time when everyone is eating too much and buying too much. We wanted to encourage them to give too much too," he said.[16]

Like Thanksgiving itself, Giving Tuesday has roots in religion.

"There was not a religious element per se when we were creating Giving Tuesday," Timms said. "But there is certainly a sense that Giving Tuesday is based on the bedrock values of the 92nd Street Y—the Jewish values of philanthropy, community, and repairing the world. We are always thinking about how we can take these values and spread them."

Giving Tuesday is best explained as a movement or a collaboration. The name is not trademarked, there are no rules for membership, and there is no central superstructure. Participation is open to all. Nonprofit organizations or groups raising money for charitable purposes simply announce to their followers that they are taking part in Giving Tuesday. Each participating group then takes its own initiative to create activities and raise money under the banner of Giving Tuesday. The organizers offer a helping hand—for example, creating a toolkit of how-to materials that they make available for partners' use. The toolkit could include model press releases, information on how to use social media effectively, online chats with fundraising experts, and so on. The organizers sought to create momentum for Giving Tuesday by encouraging donors to use social media to talk about the causes they believe in and the organizations they support.

Giving Tuesday caught on quickly. The goal was to have one hundred participants in the first year, but more than two thousand five hundred organizations took part, across all fifty states. Three years later, in 2015, Giving Tuesday raised $116.7 million from nearly seven hundred thousand donors at ten thousand participating organizations.

That same year, Giving Tuesday had partners in seventy-one countries, where the idea resonates on its own, with no connection to the American Thanksgiving holiday. "We originally thought Giving Tuesday only made sense in the context of Thanksgiving," Timms said. "We were wrong."

America's Thanksgiving holiday may not be observed overseas, but the Thanksgiving spirit is catching on worldwide.

CHAPTER TEN

Turkey Day

No citizen of the United States should refrain from Turkey on Thanksgiving Day.
— attributed to Alexander Hamilton[1]

For more than two hundred years, Americans have been sitting down to the same meal on Thanksgiving Day: roast turkey with stuffing, cranberry sauce, potatoes, and one or more kinds of pie. According to a recent survey, an astonishing 88 percent of Americans eat turkey for Thanksgiving dinner. Forty-six million turkeys help Americans celebrate their favorite holiday.[2]

To be sure, there are regional and ethnic variations in Thanksgiving Day menus. Southerners might stuff their turkey with cornbread; New Englanders will choose a bread stuffing seasoned with celery, sage, and onion; and Asian Americans might prefer a rice-based one. Pumpkin, mince, apple, and pecan pie all have their own fans and compete for space on the dessert table.

Culinary fashions have come and gone over the years; oysters and chicken pie, staples of Thanksgiving dinner for much of the nineteenth century, aren't often seen on holiday tables today. And in the twenty-first century, who has heard of Marlborough pie, a colonial favorite? But the basic bill of fare that defines the traditional New England Thanksgiving repast has been gracing holiday tables since at least the eighteenth century.

That menu is such a culinary fixture that some might be surprised to learn that it bears little resemblance to the meal shared by the Pilgrims and the Wampanoag at their three-day celebration in 1621. Legend has it that they ate turkey, and it is appealing to imagine that generations of Americans have been eating turkey in solidarity with those who sat down to the original Thanksgiving feast. While it is possible that turkey was on the table, there is, alas, no concrete evidence for it. If twenty-first-century diners want to be sure they are eating what our forefathers and foremothers feasted on so long ago at the First Thanksgiving, they would need to stock up on venison, mussels, corn, and squash.

In his eyewitness account of the occasion, Edward Winslow mentions that the governor sent four men hunting. The quartet bagged a large number of fowl—enough to feed the settlers for almost a week, Winslow writes. He doesn't specify what kind of fowl, or, more to the point, whether the birds included turkeys.

William Bradford's own depiction of the First Thanksgiving offers a more explicit hint that turkey may have been part of the feast, as we saw earlier. Bradford writes: "There was a great store of wild turkeys, of which they took many." The woods of New England were full of wild turkey in the early seventeenth century, and it makes sense to presume that turkeys were part of the 1621 feast, though we can't know for sure. There is no indication that turkey occupied the dominant place in the meal that it does today.

Other fowl were more likely to have been on the menu. Duck and geese were so plentiful in the fall that hunters could position themselves in a marsh and fire at dozens of birds floating on the water. There are contemporaneous accounts of the early settlers of New England eating swan, crane, and even eagle. As for stuffing, cooks back in England roasted their fowl with herbs and onions inside the cavity, and it is probable that Pilgrim chefs would have followed suit in Plymouth.[3]

We know, too, that venison was a prominent feature of the original feast. Winslow states that Massasoit and his warriors presented five deer they had killed to Governor Bradford and Captain Myles Standish. This gift would have provided several meals for the fifty-three Pilgrims and their ninety guests.

Seafood, which was readily available in the waters near Plymouth, would also have played a large role. Bradford writes about fishing for cod and bass. Winslow describes how Plymouth Bay was "full of lobsters" and a "variety of other fish." Eels were easy to catch, and mussels were "at our door." Oysters weren't readily available in Plymouth Bay but could be obtained from local Indians, Winslow says. He also mentions grapes, strawberries, gooseberries, raspberries, and three kinds of plums—all of which could have been picked in the summer, dried, and stored for winter eating.

It is easier for culinary historians to determine what was *not* served at the First Thanksgiving than to figure out what was actually on the menu. Several now-traditional foods were not available in New England in the 1620s, among them cranberry sauce, white potatoes, sweet potatoes, and apples.

Cranberries would have grown wild near Plymouth, ripening in the fall, but if a curious Pilgrim had picked and eaten one berry, he would not have wanted to eat a second. Cranberries are extremely tart and need sweetening to be palatable. Since sugar was very expensive in England, the Pilgrims were unlikely to have brought any with them on the *Mayflower*. It would be half a century before an English writer would mention boiling cranberries with sugar to make a sauce to accompany meat. Indians used dried cranberries as seasoning, and it is possible the Pilgrims adopted that practice and added dried berries to a dish served at the First Thanksgiving.

White potatoes, which originated in South America, did not grow in New England, and the Wampanoag were not familiar with them. Although white potatoes had been exported to Europe, they were not generally accepted as part of the English diet at the time. Sweet potatoes came from the Caribbean and the Spanish had adopted them, but they were rare in England, where they were considered a luxury and an aphrodisiac. The Pilgrims were unlikely to have tasted them.

Apples also were unknown in the New World in 1621. It wouldn't be long before colonists planted imported apple seeds, but the fruit itself wasn't available until the end of the seventeenth century. Despite the saying "as American as apple pie," there is nothing indigenous to the land now called the United States of America in that popular dessert.

Speaking of pie, that too was missing, which meant there was no pumpkin pie at the First Thanksgiving. The Pilgrims surely were familiar with pie, which was commonplace back home, and pumpkins were native to New England. But they would not have been able to put the two together at the time of the First Thanksgiving for the simple reason that they lacked butter and wheat flour for making piecrust. If the Pilgrims served pumpkin at the First Thanksgiving, it would have been in the form of pudding or stew.

The trio of native vegetables known as the Three Sisters were surely on the menu as representative of the harvest the Pilgrims were celebrating. The Three Sisters—corn, squash, and beans—were staples of the Indians' diet and were adopted by the Pilgrims. Per the Indian custom, the three vegetables were planted together. As food writer Libby O'Connell explained in her book, *The American Plate*, "The tendrils of the bean plant climbed up the cornstalk, supporting both the bean and corn plants, while the large flat leaves of the squash plant discouraged weeds."[4] The Three Sisters combined as well in the bowl as they did in the field. Corn is nutritionally incomplete, but in combination with beans it makes a complete protein. This was the basic form of succotash.

There is scant information about what New Englanders ate on days of thanksgiving in the seventeenth and early eighteenth centuries. One account from 1714 mentions a "bountiful" dinner with bear meat and venison.[5]

From Georgia comes a record of a dinner held in November 1732 in connection with a day of thanksgiving. The first English settlers there, led by James Oglethorpe, had a feast on the Sunday after their arrival. One hundred thirty people dined on "four fat hogs, eight turkeys, besides chickens and beef, [and] drank one hogshead of punch, one of beer, and a vast deal of wine." (A hogshead is about sixty-four gallons.) The following year, the town of Savannah gave thanks on July 7 with a "very substantial dinner."[6]

By the second half of the eighteenth century, reports of Thanksgiving dinner in New England begin to appear more frequently. A minister's daughter named Juliana Smith in Sharon, Connecticut, vividly sketched her family's Thanksgiving dinner in a letter to her cousin Betsey in 1779.[7] The War of Independence was raging, so "of course, we could have no roast beef," she wrote. "None of us have tasted beef these three years back as it all must go to the army, & too little they get, poor fellows." Instead, like the Pilgrims and the Wampanoag in 1621, the Smith family ate venison. As was also the case at the First Thanksgiving, the Smiths' venison came courtesy of a local Native American, from whom the family purchased "a fine red deer."

It was Uncle Simeon's turn to host the Smith family's Thanksgiving dinner, and Juliana described for her cousin both the meal and how it was served. A haunch of venison was placed on one end of each of the two tables in the dining room of her uncle's house. At the other end of each table was a huge cut, or "chine," of roast pork. One table held a large roast turkey; the other had a goose. Each table also had a huge pigeon pastie, or pie. There was an assortment of vegetables,

including one that Juliana thought her cousin had never seen: "sell-
ery," or celery in today's spelling. "You eat it without cooking," she
explained. "It is very good served with meats."

For dessert, the Smith family served mince pie, pumpkin pie, apple
tarts, and Indian puddings. Suet pudding stood in for the traditional
plum pudding and was made with a jar of West Indian preserved ginger that was left over from a shipment that the family had received
before the war began and the British blockaded American ports. The
baking of the pies and cakes occupied three days, Juliana wrote, and
the ladies "had to do without some things that ought to be used" due
to the war. They substituted dried cherries for raisins, which "neither
love nor money could buy." The family also did without wine. Uncle
Simeon still had a "cask or two" from before the war, but it had to be
saved for the sick. No matter. Juliana was a good patriot and did not
complain: "Good cider is a sufficient substitute," she reasoned.

Another glimpse of a New England Thanksgiving dinner in the eighteenth century comes courtesy of the *Connecticut Courant*. In 1792, the
newspaper published a letter from an anonymous correspondent whose
reflections on the culinary habits that prevailed on Thanksgiving Day
provide a window on what New Englanders considered to be the appropriate holiday fare.[8] The correspondent offered his personal estimates of
the amounts of holiday food consumed by the 685,000 residents of Connecticut, Massachusetts, and Rhode Island. They included:

★ 40,000 plum puddings
★ 85,694 turkeys or geese

* 128,541 chicken pies
* 514,164 mince pies
* 514,164 apple pies
* 257,082 rice or potato pies
* 1,028,328 pumpkin pies

A word here about chicken pie. It is not a dish that modern cooks associate with Thanksgiving dinner, but it used to be a staple of the New England holiday meal. From a modern-day perspective, it would seem an odd choice. Chicken pies are homely fare, a kind of colonial comfort food. They would have been familiar to every New Englander, and also to the transplanted children of New England in other parts of the expanding country. Chicken pies may have earned their place on the Thanksgiving table for reasons of nostalgia, bringing back sweet memories of home.

Colonial wives baked chicken pies for practical reasons. They were nutritious, filling, and relatively inexpensive, since every farm wife kept chickens. For the colonists, a piecrust was easy to prepare. It did not require a brick oven for baking, and it needed less flour than bread. There are early New England recipes for other kinds of savory pies— among them seafood, partridge, pigeon, goose, quail, veal, mutton, and beef tongue. But chicken pie remained the Thanksgiving favorite, and it graced holiday tables into the early years of the twentieth century.

An excellent indication of the kinds of dishes American cooks were preparing in the eighteenth century comes from the first American cookbook, *American Cookery*, by Amelia Simmons.[9] It was published in two editions in 1796—one in Hartford, Connecticut, and another in Albany, New York. Before *American Cookery*, the only cookbooks available in the United States were English and pertained to foods that were available in England. *American Cookery* was the first cookbook to include recipes for foods that were commonplace in the United States, such as pumpkin, squash, and especially Indian corn, which colonial cooks used heavily. No English cookbook told Americans how to cook with cornmeal. Simmons provided five recipes that used it.

American Cookery contains "receipts," or recipes, for many Thanksgiving favorites. There are several for turkey, including one with cranberry sauce, which may be the first recorded recipe for that pairing. *American Cookery*'s recipe for turkey stuffing calls for bread, beef suet, eggs, thyme, marjoram, salt, pepper, and a "gill" (about four ounces) of wine. Take away the suet, and the recipe is similar to those used today. There are also recipes for numerous dessert pies, including mince and apple as well as several for the ever-popular *pompkin* or pumpkin. The spices used with pumpkin—mace, nutmeg, ginger—will be familiar to the modern-day baker. Indian pudding, a classic New England dessert made with cornmeal and molasses, rates three recipes.

An entire chapter of Sarah Josepha Hale's novel, *Northwood*, published in 1827, is devoted to a detailed description of a New England Thanksgiving dinner. Hale, who was born in 1788, based her fictional account on childhood memories of growing up in rural New Hampshire.

In Hale's telling, the turkey was the king of the day: "The roasted turkey took precedence on this occasion, being placed at the head of the table," she wrote, "and well did it become its lordly station, sending forth the rich odor of its savory stuffing, and finely covered with the froth of the basting."[10]

Like Juliana Smith's description of her Thanksgiving dinner in 1779, the menu of Hale's fictional dinner was heavy on meat. Opposite the turkey, at the foot of the table, was "a sirloin of beef, flanked on either side by a leg of pork and loin of mutton." Also on the table were a goose, two ducklings, and an enormous chicken pie, "formed of the choicest parts of fowls, enriched and seasoned with a profusion of butter and pepper, and covered with an excellent puff paste." She hailed the chicken pie as "an indispensable part of a good and true Yankee Thanksgiving."

That was the first course. The second course—dessert—was arrayed on a heavily laden sideboard. There were a huge plum pudding, "custards and pies of every name and description," several kinds of cake, and a variety of fruits. Among all these, the "celebrated" and also "indispensable" pumpkin pie "occupied the most distinguished niche." There were drinks on the sideboard, too: currant wine, cider, and ginger beer. All the beverages were homemade; no imported wine or spirits were offered. At the conclusion of the meal, the sated diners were "sorrowful" that they could not eat more.

If the turkey was the king of the day, to use Hale's encomium, pies were the queen. In her 1869 novel, *Oldtown Folks*, Harriet Beecher Stowe wrote about the "endless array of pies" at Thanksgiving dinner. In their "tempting variety," they "bewildered" and "overpowered" the diner. The making of pies, she wrote, assumed vast proportions that verged on the sublime. Pies were made by the forties and fifties and hundreds, and made of everything on the earth and under the sun.... Pumpkin pies, cranberry pies, huckleberry pies, cherry pies, green currant pies, peach, pear and plum pies, custard pies, apple pies, Marlborough-pudding pies, pies with top crusts, pies without, pies adorned with all sorts of fanciful fluting and architectural strips laid across and around, and otherwise varied, attested to the boundless fertility of the feminine mind, when once let loose in a given direction.[11]

A century after Stowe, one of America's foremost food writers, the delightfully named Clementine Paddleford, also sang the praises of Thanksgiving pies. "Tell me where your grandmother came from," Paddleford wrote in her 1960 book, *How America Eats*, "and I can tell you how many kinds of pie you serve for Thanksgiving."[12] In the Midwest, two pies is the norm, Paddleford observed—pumpkin and mince. In the East, it is a threesome: pumpkin, mince, and cranberry. Many Southern hostesses prefer to serve wine jelly on Thanksgiving, she said, though other experts might disagree, referencing two Southern favorites, sweet potato pie and pecan pie. There was also an etiquette pertaining to Thanksgiving pies, Paddleford explained. In colonial times it was thought "penurious and incorrect to offer company fewer than three kinds of pie."[13]

Paddleford traveled the country in her research for *How America Eats*, interviewing women whose families had lived in particular communities for generations and coaxing family recipes and culinary lore out of them. In New Hampshire, she learned about early pumpkin pies. They were "queer" things, made by cutting a hole in the pumpkin, scooping out the seeds, and stuffing the cavity with a mixture of apples, spices, sugar, and milk. The "plug" was then returned to the hole and the filled pumpkin was baked.[14]

Paddleford heard hostesses dismiss apple pie as too everyday to serve for Thanksgiving dinner. But Marlborough pie, well, that was a different story. It was a colonial favorite—a fancier kind of apple pie made with lemon and custard and baked without a top crust. Marlborough pie was considered special enough for the holiday table.

Wild turkeys are a familiar sight in New England today, but that has not always been so. They were abundant when the *Mayflower* arrived in 1620, and the colonists freely exploited a source of food that may have seemed inexhaustible. At the same time, loggers and farmers clearing land for planting whittled away at the turkey's woodland habitat. By the nineteenth century, wild turkeys were becoming rare. The last one was observed in Connecticut in 1813, in Vermont in 1842, in New York in 1844, and in Massachusetts in 1847. Wild turkey populations in the Midwest and the West disappeared by around the beginning of the twentieth century, and they were on the decline in the South also. Some observers predicted that they would soon be completely extinct in North America. After the last known passenger pigeon in the wild was shot by a young boy in 1900, many thought the wild turkey would be the next to go.[15]

As the number of turkeys in the wild diminished, the number of domesticated turkeys in the barnyard skyrocketed. Domesticated turkeys first appeared in Massachusetts in 1629, brought over from England. By the early nineteenth century, farm-raised turkeys showed up on America's table in large quantities, according to Andrew F. Smith, a food historian.[16] By the end of that century, the price of turkey had fallen to a point where it was affordable to a wide swath of the population, and eating it on Thanksgiving was so commonplace that "Turkey Day" became a synonym for the holiday. As the *Memphis Daily Appeal* put it in 1877, "a Thanksgiving dinner is scarcely complete without a turkey."

Still, not every American could afford a turkey. Witness the wistful item published the day after Thanksgiving 1886 in the *Daily Tombstone* of Tombstone, Arizona:

> The publisher of The Tombstone, and its editor, ate chuck beef steak for their Thanksgiving dinner yesterday, while a large number of delinquent subscribers to this paper dined on roast turkey. We hope that they will remember us in time to purchase a turkey for Christmas.[17]

Since the *Tombstone* ceased publication a few weeks later, history does not record whether the editor and publisher were finally able to eat the turkey dinner they longed for.

Americans who couldn't afford turkey celebrated the holiday with cheaper substitutes such as beef, pork, or possibly chicken. In 1901, the *San Francisco Call* published a low-cost Thanksgiving menu that it promised would leave "no bitter taste of unpaid bills in its wake."

In lieu of turkey, the *Call* recommended the substitution of more affordable main dishes such as chicken pie, chicken fricassee, roast spare ribs, or roast duck. Mashed potatoes, turnips, celery, cranberries, and pumpkin pie were included on the budget menu, which would serve six people at a total cost of $1.88. The leftover twelve cents could be used to buy "three pretty chrysanthemums for the center of the table."[18]

In 1914, a reporter for the *Star-Independent* newspaper in Harrisburg, Pennsylvania, covered a local farmers' market two days before Thanksgiving. He made reference to "persons with non-turkey pocketbooks." Those who could not afford the "luxury" of a turkey, he advised, could purchase a chicken or oysters for the holiday dinner.[19]

One person who never had to worry about whether he could afford a turkey was the president of the United States. In 1873, Henry Vose, the so-called poultry king of Rhode Island, began to supply Thanksgiving turkeys to the White House, the start of a forty-year tradition. The first president to receive one of Vose's renowned fowls was Ulysses S. Grant. The tradition continued until Vose's death in 1913, when Woodrow Wilson was president.

Subsequent presidents continued to receive turkeys as gifts. In the early 1920s, a Chicago girls' club sent Warren Harding a prize turkey that they had fattened up on chocolates. Harding's successor, Calvin Coolidge, received turkeys, quail, ducks, geese, rabbits, and a deer. The Coolidge family were the recipients, too, of the oddest gift intended for a First Family's Thanksgiving dinner. In 1926, a raccoon arrived at the White House from Mississippi along with the sender's assurances that the animal had a "toothsome flavor." The Coolidges declined to eat the Thanksgiving raccoon and instead turned it into a pet, which they named Rebecca.[20]

If the president of the United States could pardon a raccoon, why not a turkey? The origin of the presidential pardon of a Thanksgiving turkey, now an annual ceremony on the White House lawn, is something of a mystery. Some trace it back to Lincoln, who is said to have issued a reprieve to a turkey named Jack that had been earmarked for Christmas dinner. When young Tad Lincoln objected, the president let Jack live. The late 1940s saw the beginning of the National Thanksgiving Turkey Presentation ceremony, in which the National Turkey Federation or another industry group donates a Thanksgiving turkey to the White House—and not so incidentally provides a nice holiday photo-op for the president. At first, the president would occasionally pardon the bird, but it wasn't until George H. W. Bush became president that the turkey pardon turned into an annual event. Bush granted the pardon as animal rights activists were picketing nearby.[21]

The American soldier can also count on a turkey dinner on Thanksgiving Day. During the Civil War, private organizations made sure that Union soldiers received a taste of home on the holiday. More recently, the federal government has provided Thanksgiving dinners for American military men and women stationed overseas. In 2015, the Pentagon's Defense Logistics Agency delivered more than fifteen thousand pounds of turkey and 1,854 pies to U.S. troops stationed in Afghanistan. The combined turkey total for U.S. troops in

Afghanistan, Iraq, Jordan, and Kuwait in that year was 51,699 pounds. Soldiers refer to the holiday as Thanksgiving in the sand.

Culinary fashions come and go, and cooks' decisions about what to serve for Thanksgiving have been influenced not only by traditions but also by public preferences and the cost and availability of ingredients.

Take oysters. They were a popular feature of Thanksgiving dinner in the nineteenth century, when they were plentiful and inexpensive on both coasts. The bivalve appeared in numerous guises on Thanksgiving menus: oysters on the half shell, oyster bisque, oyster stew, oyster stuffing. The country's oyster mania lasted well into the twentieth century even though supplies had diminished sharply, and recipes for Thanksgiving dishes made with oysters continued to be popular. In 1954, the Department of the Interior issued a press release calling oysters "a Thanksgiving Day tradition" and including several recipes from the home economists of the Fish and Wildlife Service.

Chestnuts were once commonly used for stuffing the turkey or roasted as an after-dinner snack. A blight in the early twentieth century killed off most of the once-plentiful American chestnut trees, and so chestnuts, like oysters, have mostly disappeared from Thanksgiving dinners. One or the other may still turn up on the menu today, but they usually fall into the category of luxuries.

In 1959, cranberries went suddenly and emphatically out of fashion. The reason was a cancer scare that erupted a couple of weeks before

Thanksgiving Day. On November 9, the secretary of health, education and welfare, Arthur Flemming, announced that a shipment of cranberries tested by the Food and Drug Administration was found to be contaminated with low levels of a weed killer that had previously been shown to cause thyroid cancer when fed to rats in large doses. The dose of the weed killer used in the animal carcinogen test was the equivalent of a person ingesting fifteen thousand pounds of cranberries every day for years.[22] Despite the infinitesimal chance of contracting cancer from eating cranberry sauce at Thanksgiving dinner, American consumers heard only the word "cancer" alongside "cranberries."

The Great Cranberry Scare was on. Flemming's announcement sparked a nationwide boycott. Some states banned cranberry sales or called for voluntary suspensions. Supermarkets and restaurants stopped selling cranberry products.

The government quickly set up an inspection program, and cranberries that had been inspected and approved began to appear in stores shortly before the holiday. On the day after Thanksgiving, the *New York Times* published a photograph of Mr. and Mrs. Flemming passing the cranberry sauce at their own holiday dinner.[23] But it was too late. Millions of Americans had already gone without cranberries that year.

Finally, there is the turkeyless Thanksgiving dinner for reasons other than cost. Long before there was Tofurkey and long before People for the Ethical Treatment of Animals began rallying under the slogan "Give turkeys something to be thankful for," vegetarians were calling for a meatless Thanksgiving.

In 1835, William Andrus Alcott, a physician and writer, announced that he was opposed to Thanksgiving dinner on medical as well as moral grounds. He dismissed Thanksgiving as "a grand New England carnival" that extended for several days as diners gorged on unhealthy luxuries, and he saw "fevers, gouts, and other diseases lying in ambush among the dishes."[24] Alcott went on to become the first president of the American Vegetarian Society. In the early twentieth century, the call for a turkey-free Thanksgiving was taken up again by two ardent vegetarians, John Harvey Kellogg, co-inventor of cornflakes, and his wife, Ella.

In 1792, a New Englander deemed Thanksgiving a "day for eating and drinking" whose chief purpose was "to gormandize."[25] Overeating is another Thanksgiving tradition that resonates across the centuries. But the larger point here is the recurring themes of abundance and prosperity. The Thanksgiving table has come to represent the natural bounty of the American continent and the energy, diligence, and creativity of the people who have developed its riches.

Norman Rockwell captured this aspect of Thanksgiving dinner in his World War II–era painting called *Freedom from Want*, which depicts Grandma carrying an enormous roast turkey to the family's dining table. The popular painting, which was published in the *Saturday Evening Post* in 1943, became a symbol of American plenty during a war in which millions of people elsewhere in the world were going hungry. Later, at a Cold War exhibition in the Soviet Union, critics condemned Rockwell's turkey as capitalist propaganda.[26]

Rockwell's painting also reflects the themes of family, friendship, and conviviality. People of all ages are chatting and smiling around the table. No one is paying attention to the turkey except for Grandpa, who will be called upon to carve it. The values of hospitality and inclusion have been hallmarks of the Thanksgiving Day meal since the Pilgrims and the Wampanoag shared their seventeenth-century feast.

In the letter she wrote to her cousin in 1779, Juliana Smith, the young minister's daughter in Connecticut, listed the relatives and friends who gathered at the Smith family's Thanksgiving dinner that year. The guests included five local orphans, five students who were unable to travel to distant homes for the holiday, the family of six that had just moved in next door, and "four old ladies who have no longer homes or children of their own." And then there was the Smith family itself, with two grandmothers and an assortment of aunts, uncles, and cousins.

Similar assemblages of family, friends, neighbors, and individuals who might otherwise find themselves alone for the holiday will be familiar to Americans today. Thanksgiving remains essentially a family holiday, but on that day, the definition of family extends to the wider community in which we live.

Edward Winslow was the first to give written expression to the Thanksgiving sentiments of hospitality and inclusion, while marveling at the bounty of his new home. In the letter to a friend in London in which he described the First Thanksgiving, the Pilgrim closed with the following thought: "And although it be not always so plentiful, as it was at this time with us, yet by the goodness of God, we are so far from want, that we often wish you partakers of our plenty." Come join us, Winslow was urging his friend. His exuberant description of the First Thanksgiving was an invitation to a New World feast.

Today, while regional and ethnic embellishments may grace individual tables, Thanksgiving dinner is essentially the same wherever Americans gather on the fourth Thursday of November. We all eat, or overeat, the same foods. As we do, we are glad that, like Winslow in 1621, by the goodness of God, we too can partake of America's plenty.

Five Kernels of Corn

ne Fourth of July in the 1980s, when I was living in Hong Kong, a writer for a local newspaper penned a column musing on the American Independence Day. Across the United States today, the columnist declared, families are celebrating the birth of their nation by sitting down to turkey dinners with all the trimmings.

The expatriate American community in what was then a British colony shared a chuckle over the Hong Kong writer's confusion about America's national holidays. There was some good-natured joshing about celebrating Thanksgiving in July by grilling turkey burgers and slathering cranberry sauce on hot dogs. The story stayed with me over the years, and I have hauled it out to amusing effect at more than one Fourth of July picnic back in the States.

But it also set me to thinking. In some sense, the Hong Kong columnist made a natural error. A non-American could be forgiven for conflating these two quintessentially American holidays. Both bind celebrants to the larger history of our nation. Thanksgiving isn't a patriotic holiday per se, but it is full of patriotic feeling as Americans join together to give thanks for shared blessings as a nation. The best expression of this aspect of Thanksgiving Day comes from Benjamin Franklin, who called Thanksgiving a day "of public Felicity," a time to express gratitude for the "full Enjoyment of Liberty, civil and religious."

Just about every country has a national day, a holiday when citizens stop to honor their constitution, celebrate a monarch's birthday, recall the day their nation was liberated from colonial rule, or otherwise pay tribute to their country's origins. The United States isn't unique in celebrating a day of independence.

But Thanksgiving is something else. Only a few countries set aside a day of national thanksgiving. Most of these holidays trace their origins back to a time when life beat to the rhythm of the agricultural cycle. Koreans celebrate the harvest festival of Chuseok with family gatherings and visits to their ancestral homes. Similarly, China's Mid-Autumn or Moon Festival is a modernized version of long-ago harvest celebrations. Germany has Erntedankfest, when churches are decorated with symbols of the harvest. The first thanksgivings in Canada were religious ceremonies celebrated by English and French explorers, but the modern Canadian Thanksgiving Day owes a debt to the American Loyalists who carried the New England custom with them when they fled to Nova Scotia at the time of the Revolutionary War. Brazil's Thanksgiving Day, which debuted in 1949, was the brainchild of that country's ambassador to the United States, who admired the American holiday. These and other thanksgivings are joyous occasions, but they say little about what it means to be Korean or Chinese, German, Canadian, or Brazilian.

In contrast, the American Thanksgiving is far more than an update of an ancient harvest festival. Thanksgiving has grown up with the country. It reflects our national identity as a grateful, generous, and inclusive people. When a twenty-first-century American takes his place at the Thanksgiving table or volunteers at a local food bank, he is part of a continuum that dates back to 1621, when the Pilgrims and the Indians shared their famous three-day feast.

As this book has recounted, the most direct influence on the development of the holiday was the religious days of thanksgiving marked in all of the American colonies. By the turn of the eighteenth century, the after-church Thanksgiving meal had taken on an identity of its own in New England, and the holiday emerged as a time for homecomings, feasting, and hospitality, in addition to the religious aspects. The Pilgrims weren't associated with Thanksgiving until the nineteenth century, after the establishment of the now mostly forgotten holiday of Forefathers Day and the emergence of the Pilgrims as icons of liberty and the forerunners of the Founding Fathers.

The story of how Thanksgiving became a national holiday is itself a classic American saga of how one enterprising, hardworking individual with a good idea can have an impact in an open, democratic society. In this case, a penniless young widow—subject to all the limitations attached to such a station in life in the early nineteenth century—rose to become the editor of the most popular magazine of her era. Sarah Josepha Hale used her position to generate grassroots support for her campaign for a national Thanksgiving, and she petitioned the most powerful men in the land to turn her vision into a reality.

In the political realm, Thanksgiving has sparked debates about core aspects of American liberty. In 1789, George Washington's call for a national Thanksgiving ignited controversy when some members of Congress believed that the new president was exercising a power that rightly belonged to the individual states. Other opponents said the Thanksgiving proposal violated the guarantee of a separation of church and state found in the First Amendment, which Congress had just debated. In the 1930s, Franklin Roosevelt's decision to change the date of Thanksgiving set off a revolt in statehouses over presidential authority, with the result that half the country celebrated on one day and half on another.

We live in a less religious age than did the Pilgrims or Washington or Mrs. Hale, but it would be a mistake to claim, as some do, that Thanksgiving is not a religious holiday. It is that rarest of religious holidays, one that all religions can, and do, celebrate. For this, as in so many other things, the nation can thank George Washington, who declared our first Thanksgiving as a nation in a proclamation that embraced people of all faiths. The Pilgrims came to our shores seeking religious freedom. On Thanksgiving Day, Americans of all faiths—and of none—can give thanks that they found it.

The rites and rituals of our Thanksgiving celebration have evolved over four centuries, and that process surely will continue. The essence of the holiday as we celebrate it today, however, is unlikely to change. Families will continue to gather together, the turkey will take pride of place on the dinner table, and the generous spirit of the American people will ensure that the poor, the sick, the imprisoned, and the lonely won't be excluded from the celebration.

Thanksgiving's religious aspects have perhaps changed the most over the centuries. In the seventeenth century, some objected when days of thanksgiving became annual events rather than days set aside to give thanks for specific blessings. They feared that thanksgiving would lose its religious meaning and the act of giving thanks would become an empty ritual. That hasn't happened. While going to church on Thanksgiving Day is no longer commonplace, God remains at the center of the celebration—in Thanksgiving week worship services, in the president's proclamation, and most of all in the private practice of thanking the Almighty around the dinner table. If there is only one day of the year that a family will say grace, it is Thanksgiving Day.

Over the years, too, Thanksgiving has resisted being wrested into something it isn't. Unlike Columbus Day, which is being reinvented as Indigenous People's Day in a growing number of locations around the country, Thanksgiving still celebrates its origins. This bucks a fad among some contemporary thinkers, especially in the academy, who view the holiday as something shameful. Instead of celebrating, they say, we should be remembering the murder and displacement of Native Americans by European colonists. This attitude is part of a sour mindset that tends to define America by its sins and failures, rather than by its virtues and overwhelming record of success. Fortunately, few Americans buy into this distorted viewpoint.

Still, in our cynical age, the wisdom embodied in the story of the First Thanksgiving can get short shrift. The Pilgrims' story teaches courage, compassion, love of liberty, and gratitude to God. It is a heroic tale about a moment in time when two disparate peoples found a way to live together in harmony and respect. We and subsequent generations of Americans can continue to learn from it and be inspired by it.

So, in closing, let me propose the revival of a Thanksgiving custom that will help us remember. It bears a curious title, "Five Kernels of Corn," which refers to the practice of placing five kernels of dried corn on the Thanksgiving table. The tradition got its start in 1820 on Forefathers Day. The occasion was the dinner that followed Daniel Webster's celebrated oration on the Pilgrims on the bicentennial of their arrival in Plymouth.

In his speech, Webster reminded his listeners that we are "not mere insulated beings, without relation to the past or the future." We must leave for future generations "some proof that we hold the blessings transmitted from our fathers in just estimation." Among the blessings he listed was a desire to promote everything that may "improve the hearts of men," a category that would surely include Thanksgiving.

At this grand dinner, held at Plymouth's imposing new courthouse (which was still under construction at the time) and served on commemorative china that had been commissioned from a kiln in Staffordshire, England, the five kernels of corn were humble reminders of the reason for the anniversary. They represented the starving time, when the Pilgrims had little to eat, and legend has it that they survived on a daily ration of five kernels of parched Indian corn.

The legend is probably untrue. There is no mention of it in Bradford's journal or other primary sources. But that didn't stop it from taking on a life of its own, and soon five kernels of corn were appearing on Thanksgiving tables across the nation. In 1898, Hezekiah Butterworth published a poem titled "Five Kernels of Corn." It concludes:

> *Five kernels of corn!*
> *Five kernels of corn!*
> *The nation gives thanks for five kernels of corn!*
> *To the Thanksgiving feast bring five kernels of corn!*

The five kernels of corn on the Thanksgiving table carry several levels of significance. They are reminders of the hardships and privations that the Pilgrims endured, and the courage with which they faced their suffering. They symbolize, too, the generosity and friendship offered by the Wampanoag people, who taught the newcomers how to plant corn, the crop that was to prove essential to the Pilgrims' survival. Finally, the five kernels of corn represent the Pilgrims' gratitude. In the usual telling of the tale, the Pilgrims were grateful even for this meager allotment of food. Led by the governor, they gave thanks together before their meal.

Shades of the Pilgrims and the Wampanoag sit today at every American's Thanksgiving table, along with the ghosts of George Washington, Abraham Lincoln, Mrs. Hale, and other figures who have enriched our Thanksgiving tradition and helped to knit us together as a nation. This history, and more, is worthy of our remembrance, with grateful hearts, on Thanksgiving Day.

WASHINGTON

FRANKLIN

STOWE

WILDER

TWAIN

READINGS FOR

Thanksgiving

Day

BRADFORD

FITZGERALD

A. ADAMS

LINCOLN

CHURCHILL

William Bradford and Edward Winslow

— 1 6 2 1 —

There are two eyewitness accounts of the First Thanksgiving. One was penned by Plymouth's governor, William Bradford, as recorded in his journal, Of Plymouth Plantation, 1620–1647.

THEY BEGAN to gather in the small harvest they had, and to fit up their houses and dwellings against winter, being all well recovered in health and strength and had all things in good plenty. For as some were thus employed in affairs abroad, others were exercised in fishing, about cod and bass and other fish, of which they took good store, of which every

 family had their portion. All the summer there was no want; and now began to come in store of fowl, as winter approached, of which this place did abound when they came first (but afterward decreased by degrees). And besides waterfowl there was

great store of wild turkeys, of which they took many, besides venison, etc. Besides, they had about a peck of meal a week to a person, or now since harvest, Indian corn to that proportion. Which made many afterwards write so largely of their plenty here to their friends in England, which were not feigned but true reports.

The second Pilgrim eyewitness account comes courtesy of Edward Winslow in *a letter to an unnamed friend in London. His letter was published in 1622 in* *a booklet titled* Mourt's Relation.

OUR HARVEST being gotten in, our governor sent four men on fowling, that so we might after a special manner rejoice together, after we had gathered the fruits of our labors; they four in one day killed as much fowl, as with a little help beside, served the Company almost a week, at which time amongst other Recreations, we exercised our Arms, many of the Indians coming amongst us, and amongst the rest their greatest king Massasoit, with some ninety men, whom for three days we entertained and feasted, and they went out and killed five Deer, which they brought to the Plantation and bestowed on our Governor, and upon the Captain and others. And although it be not always so plentiful, as it was at this time with us, yet by the goodness of God, we are so far from want, that we often wish you partakers of our plenty.

Psalm 100, from the Ainsworth Psalter

— 1612 —

The Pilgrims were enthusiastic psalm singers. One of the books they brought *with them to Plymouth was titled* The Book of Psalmes: Englished Both in Prose and Metre with Annotations, *more commonly called the* *Ainsworth Psalter. Written by Henry Ainsworth, a Separatist clergyman,* *and published in Amsterdam in 1612, it included psalm translations both in straight prose and in metrical versions for singing, along with tunes. Here are the words to the familiar Psalm 100, one of the great songs of Thanksgiving, as the Pilgrims would have spoken them. In an annotation, Ainsworth notes that this psalm is "for the public praise of God, with thanks for his mercies."*

PSALM 100
A psalm for confession

1. Shout ye triumphantly to Jehovah all the earth.

2. Serve ye Jehovah with gladness. Come before him with singing-joy.

3. Know ye, that Jehovah *is* God.

4. Enter ye his gates, with confession; his courts with praise; confess ye to him, bless his name.

5. For Jehovah *is* good, his mercy *is* for ever: & his faith, unto generation & generation.

Private Joseph Plumb Martin,
Lieutenant Ebenezer Wild
— 1777 —

During the Revolutionary War, the Continental Congress declared December 18, 1777 to be a day of "Solemn Thanksgiving and Praise." A soldier in Washington's army, Private Joseph Plumb Martin, later wrote this bitter account of the holiday.

WE HAD NOTHING to eat for two or three days previous, except what the trees of the fields and forests afforded us. But we must now have what Congress said—a sumptuous thanksgiving to close the year of high living we had now nearly seen brought to a close. Well—to add something extraordinary to our present stock of provisions—our coun-try, ever mindful of its suffering army, opened her sympathizing heart so wide, upon this occasion, as to give us something to make the world stare. And what do you think it was, reader?—Guess.—You cannot guess, be you as much of a Yankee as you will. I will tell you: it gave each and every man *half* a *gill* of rice and a *table spoon full* of vinegar!!

After we had made sure of this extraordinary superabundant dona-tion, we were ordered out to attend a meeting and hear a sermon deliv-ered upon the occasion.... I heard a sermon, a "thanks-giving sermon," what sort of one I do not know now, nor did I at the time I heard it. I had something else to think upon; my belly put me in remembrance of the fine thanksgiving dinner I was to partake of when I could get it.... So I had nothing else to do but to go home and make out my supper as usual, upon a leg of nothing and no turnips.

Another soldier, Lieutenant Ebenezer Wild, wrote an account in his diary of his meager Thanksgiving dinner in 1777.

WE SHOULD have moved to day, but this being the day set apart by the Congress for a day of public thanksgiving, the troops are ordered to lay still; and the Caplens [chaplains] of the different Brigades to perform divine services, and officers and soldiers are desired to attend. We had no Chaplin in our brigade, and we had but a poor thanksgiving—nothing but fresh beef & flour to eat, without any salt, & but very scant of that.

Shortly after Thanksgiving Day, Martin and Wild, along with their regiments, entered Valley Forge, where they would pass the winter.

Benjamin Franklin

— c. 1 7 8 5 —

Benjamin Franklin imagines a Pilgrim "Farmer of plain Sense" who spoke out on the value of a Thanksgiving Day and urged his fellow Pilgrims to count their blessings even in the midst of hardships. The Founding Father calls Thanksgiving a day of "public Felicity," in which Americans give thanks, above all, for our "full Enjoyment of Liberty, civil and religious."

AT LENGTH, when it was proposed in the Assembly to proclaim another Fast, a Farmer of plain Sense rose and remark'd, that the Inconveniencies they suffer'd, and concerning which they had so often weary'd Heaven with their Complaints, were not so great as they might have expected, and were diminishing every day as the Colony strengthen'd; that the Earth began to reward their Labour and furnish liberally for their Subsistence; that their Seas and Rivers were full of Fish, the Air sweet, the Climate healthy; and above all, that they were there in the full Enjoyment of Liberty, civil and religious. He therefore thought that reflecting and conversing on these Subjects would be more comfortable as leading more to make them contented with their Situation; and that it would be more becoming the Gratitude they ow'd to the divine Being, if *instead of a Fast they should proclaim a Thanksgiving.* His Advice was taken, and from that day to this, they have in every Year observ'd Circumstances of public Felicity sufficient to furnish Employment for a *Thanksgiving Day*, which is therefore constantly ordered and religiously observed.

George Washington
— 1789 —

The first presidential proclamation was issued by George Washington on October 3, 1789, calling for a national Thanksgiving. His proclamation was published in newspapers throughout the new country and read from church pulpits.

THANKSGIVING DAY 1789
By the President of the United States of America
A PROCLAMATION

Whereas it is the duty of all Nations to acknowledge the providence of almighty God, to obey his will, to be grateful for his benefits, and humbly to implore his protection and favor—and Whereas both Houses of Congress have by their joint Committee requested me "to recommend to the People of the United States a day of public thanksgiving and prayer to be observed by acknowledging with grateful hearts the many signal favors of Almighty God, especially by affording them an opportunity peaceably

to establish a form of government for their safety and happiness."

Now therefore I do recommend and assign Thursday the 26th day of November next to be devoted by the People of these States to the service of that great and glorious Being, who is the beneficent Author of all the good that was, that is, or that will be—That we may then all unite in rendering unto him our sincere and humble thanks—for his kind care and protection of the People of this country previous to their becoming a Nation—for the signal and manifold mercies, and the favorable interpositions of his providence, which we experienced in the course and conclusion of the late war—for the great degree of tranquility, union, and plenty, which we have since enjoyed—for the peaceable and rational manner in which we have been enabled to establish constitutions of government for our safety and happiness, and particularly the national One now lately instituted, for the civil and religious liberty with which we are blessed, and the means we have of acquiring and diffusing useful knowledge; and in general for all the great and various favors which he hath been pleased to confer upon us.

And also that we may then unite in most humbly offering our prayers and supplications to the great Lord and Ruler of Nations and beseech him to pardon our national and other transgressions—to enable us all, whether in public or private stations, to perform our several and relative duties properly and punctually—to render our national government a blessing to all the People, by constantly being a government of wise, just, and constitutional laws, discreetly and faithfully executed and obeyed—to protect and guide all Sovereigns and Nations (especially such as have shewn kindness unto us) and to bless them with good government, peace, and concord—To promote the knowledge and practice of true religion and virtue, and the increase of science among them and Us—and generally to grant unto all mankind such a degree of temporal prosperity as he alone knows to be best.

Given under my hand at the City of New York the third day of October in the year of our Lord 1789.

Go. Washington

Abigail Adams
— 1 7 9 8 —

First Lady Abigail Adams, at home alone in Quincy, Massachusetts, on Thanksgiving Day 1798, wrote to her husband, President John Adams, in Philadelphia, the temporary capital of the United States while Washington, D.C. and the White House were being built.

 Quincy, Nov'br 29, 1798

My dearest friend

This is our Thanksgiving day. When I look Back upon the Year past, I perceive many, very many causes for thanksgiving, both of a publick and private nature. I hope my Heart is not ungratefull, tho sad; it is usually a day of festivity when the Social Family circle meet together tho seperated the rest of the year. No Husband dignifies my Board, no Children add gladness to it, no Smiling Grandchildren Eyes to sparkle for the plumb pudding, or feast upon the mind Eye. Solitary and alone I behold the day after a sleepless night, without a joyous feeling. Am I ungratefull? I hope not. Brother Cranchs illness prevented Him and my sister from joining me, and Boylston Adams's sickness confineing him to his House debared me from inviting your Brother and Family. I had but one [resource] and that was to invite Mr. and Mrs. Porter to dine with me: and the two Families to unite in the Kitchin with Pheby the only surviving parent I have, and thus we shared in the Bounties of providence.

I was not well enough to venture to meeting and by that means lost an excellent discourse deliverd by Mr. Whitman upon the numerous causes of thankfullness and gratitude which we all have to the Great Giver of every perfect Gift; . . .

I presume you reachd Philadelphia on Saturday. I wrote to you twice to N York to the care of Charles and twice I have written to you addrest to Philadelphia. I hope you received the Letters.

I am as ever Your truly affectionate

A Adams

In his reply, dated December 13, 1798, John Adams begged his wife to "banish as much as possible all gloomy Thoughts."

Daniel Webster

— 1820 —

Forefathers Day, a holiday that sprang up in the eighteenth century in obser-
vation of the anniversary of the Pilgrims' arrival at Plymouth, is one of the
influences on the modern-day celebration of Thanksgiving, which includes

recognition of the role of the Pilgrims and the Indians. Daniel Webster's Fore-fathers Day oration of 1820, the bicentennial of the landing of the Pilgrims, did much to bring the Pilgrims to the attention of Americans. He praised their courage, fortitude, and attachment to the "principles of civil and religious liberty," including the rule of law and property rights. In this passage, which comes near the beginning of the speech, he urged Americans to remember their inheritance. The Pilgrims eventually became integral to Thanksgiving celebrations.

LET US REJOICE that we behold this day. Let us be thankful that we have lived to see the bright and happy breaking of the auspicious morn...the dawn that awakens us to the commemoration of the landing of the Pilgrims....

We live in the past by a knowledge of its history; and in the future, by hope and anticipation. By ascending to an association with our ancestors; by contemplating their example and studying their character; by partaking their sentiments, and imbibing their spirit; by accompanying them in their toils, by sympathizing in their sufferings, and rejoicing in their successes and their triumphs; we seem to belong to their age, and to mingle our own existence with theirs. We become their contemporaries, live the lives which they lived, endure what they endured, and partake in the rewards which they enjoyed.

Nathaniel Hawthorne

— 1824, 1842 —

In November 1824, while he was a student at Bowdoin College, twenty-year-old Nathaniel Hawthorne was unable to go home for Thanksgiving. He wrote to his aunt in Salem, Massachusetts:

THE WEATHER has lately been very cold, and there is now snow enough to make some sleighing. I keep excellent fires, and do not stir from them, unless when it is absolutely necessary. I wish that I could be at home to Thanksgiving, as I really think that your puddings and pies and turkeys are superior to anybody's else. But the term does not close till about the first of January.

Almost two decades later, in 1842, Hawthorne spent a happier Thanksgiving together with his new wife, Sophia Peabody, whom he had married a few months earlier. He wrote in his journal:

THIS IS Thanksgiving Day—a good old festival; and my wife and I have kept it with our hearts, and besides have made good cheer upon our turkey, and pudding, and pies, and custards, although none sat at our board but our two selves. There was a new and livelier sense, I think, that we have at last found a home, and that a new family has been gathered since the last Thanksgiving Day.

Sarah Josepha Hale

— 1 8 2 7 —

Sarah Josepha Hale's 1827 novel Northwood *foreshadowed the author's campaign to make Thanksgiving a national holiday. Her vivid description of a New England Thanksgiving dinner is based on childhood memories of Thanksgiving Days in New Hampshire in the late eighteenth century.*

SELDOM WERE the junior members of the family allowed the high privilege of stepping on the carpet, excepting at the annual festival; and their joy at the approaching feast was considerably heightened by the knowledge that it would be holden in the best room.

The table, covered with a damask cloth...was now intended for the whole household, every child having a seat on this occasion; and the more the better, it being considered an honor for a man to sit down to his Thanksgiving dinner surrounded by a large family. The provision is always sufficient for a multitude, every farmer in the country being, at this season of the year, plentifully supplied, and every one proud of displaying his abundance and prosperity.

The roasted turkey took precedence on this occasion, being placed at the head of the table; and well did it become its lordly station, sending forth the rich odor of its savory stuffing, and finely covered with the froth of the basting. At the foot of the board, a sirloin of beef, flanked on either side by a leg of pork and loin of mutton, seemed placed as a bastion to defend innumerable bowls of gravy and plates of vegetables disposed in that quarter. A goose and pair of ducklings occupied side stations on the table; the middle being graced, as it always is on such occasions, by that rich burgomaster of the provisions, called a chicken pie. This pie, which is wholly formed of the choicest parts of fowls, enriched and seasoned with a profusion of butter and pepper, and covered with an excellent puff paste, is, like the celebrated pumpkin pie, an indispensable part of a good and true Yankee Thanksgiving; the size of the pie usually denoting the gratitude of the party who prepares the feast. The one now displayed could never have had many peers....

Plates of pickles, preserves and butter, and all the necessaries for increasing the seasoning of the viands to the demand of each palate, filled the interstices on the table, leaving hardly sufficient room for the plates of the company, a wine glass and two tumblers for each, with a slice of wheat bread lying on one of the inverted tumblers. A side table was literally loaded with the preparations for the second course, placed there to obviate the necessity of leaving the apartment during the repast....

There was a huge plum pudding, custards and pies of every name and description ever known in Yankee land; yet the pumpkin pie occupied the most distinguished niche. There were also several kinds of rich cake, and a variety of sweetmeats and fruits.

Charles Francis Adams

— 1828 —

Charles Francis Adams, son of John Quincy Adams and grandson of John Adams and Abigail Adams, spent a dull Thanksgiving Day in 1828 at the home of his future wife, Abigail Brooks. His diary entry for the day is a reminder that the family dynamics at play on Thanksgiving Day can pose challenges.

Thursday, 27th.

MORNING DULL and gloomy. Clouds very heavy. After breakfast, I rode to Medford, the weather being rather cool. Went to Meeting with the family and heard Mr. Stetson preach a Sermon of very considerable violence in a political way. He was very warm indeed and rather unnecessarily severe. As usual there was a family dinner. Mr. and Mrs. Edward Brooks, Mr. and Mrs. Frothingham, Gorham and Horatio, besides the members of the family and a multitude of children. All this was a bore to me and not half so agreeable as a plain, common Sunday would have been when I might have had Abby all to myself, but when Mr. Brooks gave me the invitation I was aware that to have declined it would have been matter of offence.

Jews of Charleston
— 1845 —

*When Governor James Hammond of South Carolina issued a Thanksgiving
proclamation in 1844 that called only on Christians to observe the day,
the Jewish community of Charleston felt wrongfully excluded, and they
protested. An article in the* Occident and American Jewish Advocate
*argued that no South Carolinian should be required to choose between
practicing his faith and "joining a universal thanksgiving for benefits
which we all have received."*

IT IS CERTAINLY surprising how difficult a thing it is to overcome
prejudice, however foolish its origin and vague its scope....

When Governor Hammond called upon the people
of his state to worship on thanksgiving day as Christians, he either meant to exclude the Jews from joining their fellow citizens in their devotions, after their
own manner, or he bid them depart from it and adopt the manner of
those who compose, as he calls it, "a Christian people." Now he must
have known that even without taking into consideration Jews, Deists,
Atheists, and Mahomedans, there are many so-called Christians in the
very state of South Carolina who do not believe in Christ as a redeemer? Did he mean to exclude them? Or did he not know when penning
his proclamation that there are many of the most enlightened men in
his own party who are *Unitarians*, or persons who deny the divinity of
Christ nearly as much as we do?... Yet these men call themselves Christians and surely would be glad to worship God on thanksgiving day....

Sarah Josepha Hale to Abraham Lincoln

— 1863 —

In the 1840s, Sarah Josepha Hale, editor of Godey's Lady's Book, *began using the pages of her popular magazine to conduct a campaign for a national Thanksgiving. In addition, she wrote hundreds of letters to politicians, businessmen, and other opinion makers seeking support for Thanksgiving. This is her letter to President Abraham Lincoln.*

Philadelphia, Sept. 28th, 1863

SIR.—

Permit me, as Editress of the "Lady's Book", to request a few minutes of your precious time, while laying before you a subject of deep interest to myself and—as I trust—even to the President of our Republic, of some importance. This subject is to have the day of our annual Thanksgiving made a National and fixed Union Festival.

You may have observed that, for some years past, there has been an increasing interest felt in our land to have the Thanksgiving held on the same day, in all the States; it now needs National recognition and authoritative fixation, only, to become permanently, an American custom and institution. Enclosed are three papers (being printed these are easily read) which will make the idea and its progress clear and show also the popularity of the plan.

For the last fifteen years I have set forth this idea in the "Lady's Book", and placed the papers before the Governors of all the States and Territories—also I have sent these to our Ministers abroad, and our Missionaries to the heathen—and commanders in the Navy. From the recipients I have received, uniformly the most kind approval. Two of these letters, one from Governor (now General) Banks and one from Governor Morgan are enclosed; both gentlemen as you will see, have nobly aided to bring about the desired Thanksgiving Union.

But I find there are obstacles not possible to be overcome without legislative aid—that each State should, by statute, make it obligatory on the Governor to appoint the last Thursday of November, annually, as Thanksgiving Day;—or, as this way would require years to be realized, it has ocurred [*sic*] to me that a proclamation from the President of the United States would be the best, surest and most fitting method of National appointment.

I have written to my friend, Hon. Wm. H. Seward, and requested him to confer with President Lincoln on this subject. As the President of the United States has the power of appointments for the District of Columbia and the Territories; also for the Army and Navy and all American citizens abroad who claim protection from the U. S. Flag—could he not, with right as well as duty, issue his proclamation for a Day of National Thanksgiving for all the above classes of persons? And would it not be fitting and patriotic for him to appeal to the Governors of all the States, inviting and commending these to unite in issuing proclamations for the last Thursday in November as the Day of Thanksgiving for the people of each State? Thus the great Union Festival of America would be established.

Now the purpose of this letter is to entreat President Lincoln to put forth his Proclamation, appointing the last Thursday in November (which falls this year on the 26th) as the National Thanksgiving for all those classes of people who are under the National Government particularly, and commending this Union Thanksgiving to each State Executive: thus, by the noble example and action of the President of the United States, the permanency and unity of our Great American Festival of Thanksgiving would be forever secured.

An immediate proclamation would be necessary, so as to reach all the States in season for State appointments, also to anticipate the early appointments by Governors.

Excuse the liberty I have taken
With profound respect
Yrs truly
Sarah Josepha Hale,
Editress of the "Lady's Book"

Abraham Lincoln

— 1 8 6 3 —

Lincoln's 1863 Thanksgiving Proclamation was the first in what has become an unbroken string of presidential Thanksgiving Proclamations. It is considered the first of our modern-day national Thanksgivings.

BY THE PRESIDENT OF THE UNITED
STATES OF AMERICA—A PROCLAMATION

The year that is drawing toward its close has been filled with the blessings of fruitful fields and healthful skies. To these bounties, which are so constantly enjoyed that we are prone to forget the source from which they come, others have been added which are of so extraordinary a nature that they can not fail to penetrate and soften even the heart which is habitually insensible to the ever watchful providence of Almighty God.

In the midst of a civil war of unequaled magnitude and severity, which has sometimes seemed to foreign states to invite and to provoke their aggression, peace has been preserved with all nations, order has been maintained, the laws have been respected and obeyed, and harmony has prevailed everywhere, except in the theater of military conflict, while that theater has been greatly contracted by the advancing armies and navies of the Union. Needful diversions of wealth and of strength from the fields of peaceful industry to the national defense have not arrested the plow, the shuttle, or the ship; the ax has enlarged the borders of our settlements, and the mines, as well of iron and coal as of the precious metals, have yielded even more abundantly than heretofore. Population has steadily increased notwithstanding the waste that has been made in the camp, the siege, and the battlefield, and the country, rejoicing in the consciousness of augmented strength and vigor, is per-

mitted to expect continuance of years with large increase of freedom. No human counsel hath devised nor hath any mortal hand worked out these great things. They are the gracious gifts of the Most High God, who, while dealing with us in anger for our sins, hath nevertheless remembered mercy.

It has seemed to me fit and proper that they should be solemnly, reverently, and gratefully acknowledged, as with one heart and one voice, by the whole American people. I do therefore invite my fellow-citizens in every part of the United States, and also those who are at sea and those who are sojourning in foreign lands, to set apart and observe the last Thursday of November next as a day of thanksgiving and praise to our beneficent Father who dwelleth in the heavens.

And I recommend to them that while offering up the ascriptions justly due to Him for such singular deliverances and blessings they do also, with humble penitence for our national perverseness and disobedience, commend to His tender care all those who have become widows, orphans, mourners, or sufferers in the lamentable civil strife in which we are unavoidably engaged, and fervently implore the interposition of the Almighty hand to heal the wounds of the nation and to restore it, as soon as may be consistent with the divine purpose, to the full enjoyment of peace, harmony, tranquillity, and union.

In testimony whereof I have hereunto set my hand and caused the seal of the United States to be affixed.

Done at the city of Washington, this 3d day of October A.D. 1863, and of the Independence of the United States the eighty-eighth.

Abraham Lincoln

Captain Andrew Upson
— 1863 —

Captain Andrew Upson of Southington, Connecticut, served in the Union Army during the Civil War. Shortly before Thanksgiving 1863, he wrote this letter on the meaning of Thanksgiving to his four children—Ida, Frank, Willie, and Mary. Three months after Thanksgiving, in February 1864, Captain Upson died from wounds received in battle.

Stevenson, Ala.

Nov. 18th, 1863

MY DEAR CHILDREN,

I suppose this letter will arrive at its destination about Thanksgiving Day—Hoping it may add to your happiness on that occasion I sit up a few moments although it is time to go to bed and every one around is asleep—Perhaps, children, you do not understand the real meaning of Thanksgiving Day—In the 1st place, you have enough to eat—That is, God has made the grain and fruits to grow during the past season, and so you have food—If now, there had been a scarcity of rain, or if war had prevailed around your home the crops would have failed—Down here there are many sections in which the corn was cut off for want of showers—In other sections it was all destroyed by the army—The people have scarcely nothing to eat—Papa has seen numbers of these people—Men, women and children—They had none of those good things that contribute to your comfort and for which you should give God thanks—

In the 2d place, you have a snug and quiet home—In this part of

the country families are often driven from their houses—They have
to leave nearly everything and flee away to strange places—Often
times women and their little ones are compelled to walk day and
night—If the weather is cold or wet they suffer much and frequently
become sick—You are not disturbed in this way and there is a reason why you should thank God who rules over all things—In the 3d
place you have books, papers, schools and various privileges which
thousands of children in other parts of the country know nothing
about—It is a bad thing to grow up in ignorance—It is a bad thing
to live where the people do not go to meeting or have good books
and maps and the means of acquiring knowledge—God has cast your
lot where you have the benefit of almost every advantage to become
learned and wise and useful—I hope you will so far understand this as
to be thankful for your opportunities and not neglect them—

Now, my children, Thanksgiving Day is appointed that we may
call to mind how much we owe to the Great and Good God—We are
very apt to think too little of our common blessings—But if they are
taken from us we begin to see their value—I hope you may never lose
your schools, or your home, or the chance of enough to eat—But none
of these things are sure to you unless it pleases God to grant them—
He has bestowed them upon you this year and the duty upon you is to
make a proper return of thanks—There is another duty—If you wish
God remember you hereafter—to give you food and clothing—friends
and all desirable blessings you must live in a way to please Him—The
wicked he punishes by cutting off their support—by withholding the
rain—by bringing upon them trouble and calamity—He will do this or

something worse to you if you break his laws—But if you obey Him—
be obedient—be merciful—be industrious—be truthful—he will certainly provide for your wants and make your lives happy—

I should like very much, Dear Children, to sit down with you at
the Thanksgiving Supper—Perhaps another year God will permit us
to meet on this anniversary—Whatever may be our condition let us
be very thankful—Papa sends his best wishes and his tender affection to each of you and also to Mother and Grandmother—

From your loving father,

Andrew Upson

*Captain Upson's Thanksgiving letter is one of more than one hundred let-
ters he wrote to his family during the Civil War. The collection belongs to
the Barnes Museum in Southington, Connecticut.*

Louisa May Alcott

— 1882 —

In her novella An Old-Fashioned Thanksgiving, *Louisa May Alcott
tells the story of a woman who must leave her family on Thanksgiving
Day to care for her ailing mother. The story is set on the Bassett farm in
New Hampshire in the 1820s. In this excerpt, Alcott sets the scene for the
holiday, in whose preparations the entire family participated.*

MANY YEARS AGO, up among the New Hampshire hills, lived Farmer Bassett, with a house full of sturdy sons and daughters growing up
about him. They were poor in money, but rich in land and love, for
the wide acres of wood, corn, and pasture land fed, warmed, and

clothed the flock, while mutual patience, affection, and courage made the old farm-house a very happy home.

November had come; the crops were in, and barn, buttery, and bin were overflowing with the harvest that rewarded the summer's hard work. The big kitchen was a jolly place just now, for in the great fire-place roared a cheerful fire; on the walls hung garlands of dried apples, onions, and corn; up aloft from the beams shone crook-

necked squashes, juicy hams, and dried venison—for in those days deer still haunted the deep forests, and hunt-ers flourished. Savory smells were in the air; on the crane hung steaming kettles, and down among the red em-bers copper saucepans simmered, all suggestive of some approaching feast.

A white-headed baby lay in the old blue cradle that had rocked seven other babies, now and then lifting his head to look out, like a round, full moon, then subsided to kick and crow contentedly, and suck the rosy apple he had no teeth to bite. Two small boys sat on the wooden settle shelling corn for popping, and picking out the biggest nuts from the goodly store their own hands had gathered in Octo-ber. Four young girls stood at the long dresser, busily chopping meat, pounding spice, and slicing apples; and the tongues of Tilly, Prue, Roxy, and Rhody went as fast as their hands. Farmer Bassett, and Eph, the oldest boy, were "chorin' 'round" outside, for Thanksgiving was at hand, and all must be in order for that time-honored day.

D. W. Bushyhead

— 1885 —

The principal chief of the Cherokee Nation, D. W. Bushyhead, signed a proclamation on November 26, 1885, declaring that Thanksgiving should be practiced by the Cherokees.

THE CHEROKEES have abundant reason to rejoice. They are favored in all things that should make a Nation prosperous and a people happy. They have an indisputable right to an area of land sufficient for the needs of generations of Cherokees to come. They have a perfect form of Government, wise laws, unsurpassed educational facilities for their children and money enough of their own invested to make these blessings permanent. It is true this Nation is neither numerous, wealthy nor powerful compared with many others, but it stands and relies upon the plighted faith of a Nation that has become the strongest on earth by reason of its respect for human rights.

Edward Everett Hale

— 1892 —

A charming description of Thanksgiving Day is found in Edward Everett Hale's 1892 memoir, A New England Boyhood. *Hale (no relation to Sarah Josepha Hale) was a Unitarian minister, historian, and writer. In his book, he describes the Thanksgiving dinners he remembers from his childhood in Boston in the 1820s.*

HAD WE CHILDREN been asked what we expected on Thanksgiving Day we should have clapped our hands and said that we expected a good dinner. As we had a good dinner every day of our lives this answer shows simply that children respect symbols and types. And indeed there were certain peculiarities in the Thanksgiving dinner which there were not on common days. For instance, there was always a great deal of talk about the Marlborough pies or the Marlborough pudding. To this hour, in any old and well-regulated family in New England, you will find there is a traditional method of making the Marlborough pie, which is a sort of lemon pie, and each good housekeeper thinks that her grandmother left a better receipt for Marlborough pie than anybody else did. We had Marlborough pies at other times, but we were sure to have them on Thanksgiving Day; and it ought to be said that there was no other day on which we had four kinds of pies on the table and plum pudding beside, not to say chicken pie. In those early days ice cream or sherbets or any other kickshaws of that variety would have been spurned from a Thanksgiving dinner. . . .

Of those first Thanksgiving Days my memories are simply of undisguised delight. I wonder now that I did not die the day after the first of them from having eaten five times as much as I should have done. But there seems to be a good Providence which watches over boys and girls, as over idiots and drunken people. This is sure, that I have survived to tell the story.

Mark Twain

— 1 9 0 7 —

*American humorist Mark Twain reflects acidly on Thanksgiving in this
excerpt from the* Autobiography of Mark Twain *(University of California Press, 2010), describing an event that took place in 1907, and published one hundred years after the writer's death.*

THANKSGIVING DAY, a function which originated in New England
two or three centuries ago when those people recognized that they really had something to be thankful for—annually, not oftener—if they
had succeeded in exterminating their neighbors, the Indians, during
the previous twelve months instead of getting exterminated by their
neighbors the Indians. Thanksgiving Day became a habit, for the reason that in the course of time, as the years drifted on, it was perceived
that the exterminating had ceased to be mutual and was all on the white
man's side, consequently on the Lord's side, consequently it was proper
to thank the Lord for it and extend the usual annual compliments.

The original reason for a Thanksgiving Day has long ago ceased to
exist—the Indians have long ago been comprehensively and satisfactori-
ly exterminated and the account closed with Heaven, with thanks due.
But, from old habit, Thanksgiving Day has remained with us, and every
year the President of the United States and the Governors of all the several states and the territories set themselves the task, every November,
to advertise for something to be thankful for, and then they put those
thanks into a few crisp and reverent phrases, in the form of a Proclama-

tion, and this is read from all the pulpits in the land, the national conscience is wiped clean with one swipe, and sin is resumed at the old stand.

Laura Ingalls Wilder
— 1916 —

Laura Ingalls Wilder, author of the children's classic, Little House on
the Prairie, *recalls a life lesson she learned from a Thanksgiving during
her childhood in the Dakota Territory during the 1870s.* The Missouri
Realist *published her recollections in 1916.*

As Thanksgiving Day draws near again, I am reminded of an oc-
currence of my childhood. To tell the truth, it is a yearly habit of mind
to think of it about this time and to smile at it once more.

We were living on the frontier in South Dakota. There's no more frontier within the boundaries of the United States, more's the pity, but then
we were ahead of the railroad in a new unsettled country. Our nearest
and only neighbor was 12 miles away and the store was 40 miles distant.

Father had laid in a supply of provisions for the winter and among
them were salt meats, but for fresh meat we depended on father's gun
and the antelope which fed in herds across the prairie. So we were
quite excited, one day near Thanksgiving, when father hurried into the
house for his gun and then went away again to try for a shot at a belated
flock of wild geese hurrying south.

We should have roast goose for Thanksgiving dinner! "Roast goose
and dressing seasoned with sage," said sister Mary. "No, not sage! I
don't like sage and we won't have it in the dressing," I exclaimed. Then

we quarreled, sister Mary and I, she insisting that there should be sage in the dressing and I declaring there should not be sage in the dressing, until father returned—without the goose!

I remember saying in a meek voice to sister Mary, "I wish I had let you have the sage," and to this day when I think of it I feel again just as I felt then and realize how thankful I would have been for roast goose and dressing with sage seasoning—with or without any seasoning—I could even have gotten along without the dressing. Just plain goose roasted would have been plenty good enough.

This little happening has helped me to be properly thankful even tho at times the seasoning of my blessings has not been just such as I would have chosen.

Winston Churchill

— 1944 —

"To You, America—A Thanksgiving Day Celebration." That was the title of the concert held on November 23, 1944 at the Royal Albert Hall in London to raise money for King George's Fund for Sailors. The American community turned out in large numbers, and the auditorium was packed when a surprise speaker took the stage. Standing under an enormous blow-up of a photograph of Lincoln, Prime Minister Winston Churchill spoke of war, peace, and a future day of Thanksgiving in which "all the world will share."

IT IS YOUR Day of Thanksgiving, and when we feel the truth of the facts which are before us, that in three or four years the peaceful, peace-loving people of the United States, with all the variety and freedom of their life in such contrast to the iron discipline which has governed many other communities—when we see that in three or four years the United States has in sober fact become the greatest military, naval, and air power in the world—that, I say to you in this time of war, is itself a subject for profound thanksgiving....

But there is a greater thanksgiving day, which still shines ahead, which beckons the bold and loyal and warm-hearted. And that is when this union of action which has been forced upon us by our common hatred of tyranny, which we have maintained during those dark and fearful days, shall become a lasting union of sympathy and feeling and loyalty and hope between all the British and American peoples, wherever they may dwell. Then, indeed, there will be a Day of Thanksgiving, and one in which all the world will share.

F. Scott Fitzgerald

— 1945 —

F. Scott Fitzgerald's amusing list of thirteen ways to use leftover Thanksgiving turkey was published in 1945 in The Crack-Up *(New Directions, 1945), a posthumous collection of some of his shorter works. "At this post holiday season," Fitzgerald wrote, "the refrigerators of the nation are overstuffed with large masses of turkey, the sight of which is calculated to give an adult an attack of dizziness." Here is one of his recipes:*

1. *Turkey Cocktail*: To one large turkey add one gallon of vermouth and a demijohn of angostura bitters. Shake.

Korean War

— 1950 —

At the time of Thanksgiving in 1950, General Douglas MacArthur, su-
preme commander of U.S. forces in the Far East, was announcing that the
U.S. troops in Korea would be home by Christmas. This is Stanley Wein-
traub's description of Thanksgiving in "the frozen, windswept north of Ko-
rea," as told in A Christmas Far from Home: An Epic Tale of Courage
and Survival During the Korean War *(Da Capo Press, 2014).*

ALMOST NOTHING kept the efficient military logistical services
from furnishing elaborate Thanksgiving dinners sometime from
Thursday through the weekend for all the troops in Korea, even if the
dinners, complete to the holiday trimmings, had to be air-dropped.
From Pusan in the south almost to the Yalu, celebrating the occasion
was a triumph of American inge-

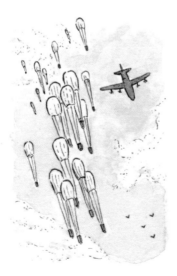

nuity. Spare parts for vehicles and
spare socks for men as well as stock-
piles of fuel and anti-freeze were
lacking, but trestle tables up and
down the peninsula were heaped
with aluminum containers of roast
turkey with gravy, cranberry sauce,
shrimp cocktail, asparagus, stewed
tomatoes, "snowflake" and candied
sweet potatoes, green peas and
whole kernel corn, stuffed olives,

sliced pineapple, fruitcake and pumpkin pie, most of it prepared in Japan from ingredients shipped from the States.

Two more Thanksgiving Days would pass before an armistice was signed in 1953.

— 1961 —

Since 1961, the Wall Street Journal *has been publishing the same two Thanksgiving editorials on the day before the holiday. Now more than a half century old, the editorials remain very popular, turning up on the newspaper's online list of most-read articles. "The Desolate Wilderness" is an excerpt from a seventeenth-century history of Plymouth. "And the Fair Land" was written by Vermont Connecticut Royster, then the* Journal's *editor.*

THE DESOLATE WILDERNESS

Here beginneth the chronicle of those memorable circumstances of the year 1620, as recorded by Nathaniel Morton, keeper of the records of Plymouth Colony, based on the account of William Bradford, sometime governor thereof:

So they left that goodly and pleasant city of Leyden, which had been their resting-place for above eleven years, but they knew that they were pilgrims and strangers here below, and looked not much on these things, but lifted up their eyes to Heaven, their dearest country, where God hath prepared for them a city (Heb. XI, 16), and therein quieted their spirits.

When they came to Delfs-Haven they found the ship and all things ready, and such of their friends as could not come with them followed after them, and sundry came from Amsterdam to see them shipt, and to take their leaves of them. One night was spent with little sleep with the most, but with friendly entertainment and Christian discourse, and other real expressions of true Christian love.

The next day they went on board, and their friends with them, where truly doleful was the sight of that sad and mournful parting, to hear what sighs and sobs and prayers did sound amongst them; what tears did gush from every eye, and pithy speeches pierced each other's heart, that sundry of the Dutch strangers that stood on the Key as spectators could not refrain from tears. But the tide (which stays for no man) calling them away, that were thus loath to depart, their Reverend Pastor, falling down on his knees, and they all with him, with watery cheeks commended them with the most fervent prayers unto the Lord and His blessing; and then with mutual embraces and many tears they took their leaves one of another, which proved to be the last leave to many of them.

Being now passed the vast ocean, and a sea of troubles before them in expectations, they had now no friends to welcome them, no inns to entertain or refresh them, no houses, or much less towns, to repair unto to seek for succour; and for the season it was winter, and they that know the winters of the country know them to be sharp and violent, subject to cruel and fierce storms, dangerous to travel to known places, much more to search unknown coasts.

Besides, what could they see but a hideous and desolate wilderness, full of wilde beasts and wilde men? and what multitudes of them there were, they then knew not: for which way soever they turned their eyes (save upward to Heaven) they could have but little solace or content in respect of any outward object; for summer being ended, all things stand in appearance with a weatherbeaten face, and the whole country, full of woods and thickets, represented a wild and savage hew.

If they looked behind them, there was a mighty ocean which they had passed, and was now as a main bar or gulph to separate them from all the civil parts of the world.

And the Fair Land

Any one whose labors take him into the far reaches of the country, as ours lately have done, is bound to mark how the years have made the land grow fruitful.

This is indeed a big country, a rich country, in a way no array of figures can measure and so in a way past belief of those who have not seen it. Even those who journey through its Northeastern complex, into the Southern lands, across the central plains and to its Western slopes can only glimpse a measure of the bounty of America.

And a traveler cannot but be struck on his journey by the thought that this country, one day, can be even greater. America, though many know it not, is one of the great underdeveloped countries of the world; what it reaches for exceeds by far what it has grasped.

So the visitor returns thankful for much of what he has seen, and, in spite of everything, an optimist about what his country might be. Yet the visitor, if he is to make an honest report, must also note the air of unease that hangs everywhere.

For the traveler, as travelers have been always, is as much questioned as questioning. And for all the abundance he sees, he finds the questions put to him ask where men may repair for succor from the troubles that beset them.

His countrymen cannot forget the savage face of war. Too often they have been asked to fight in strange and distant places, for no clear purpose they could see and for no accomplishment they can measure. Their spirits are not quieted by the thought that the good and pleasant bounty that surrounds them can be destroyed in an instant by a single bomb. Yet they find no escape, for their survival and comfort now depend on unpredictable strangers in far-off corners of the globe.

How can they turn from melancholy when at home they see young arrayed against old, black against white, neighbor against neighbor, so that they stand in peril of social discord. Or not despair when they see that the cities and countryside are in need of repair, yet find themselves threatened by scarcities of the resources that sustain their way of life. Or when, in the face of these challenges, they turn for leadership to men in high places—only to find those men as frail as any others.

So sometimes the traveler is asked whence will come their succor. What is to preserve their abundance, or even their civility? How can they pass on to their children a nation as strong and free as the one they inherited from their forefathers? How is their country to endure these cruel storms that beset it from without and from within?

Of course the stranger cannot quiet their spirits. For it is true that everywhere men turn their eyes today much of the world has a truly wild and savage hue. No man, if he be truthful, can say that the specter of war is banished. Nor can he say that when men or communities are put upon their own resources they are sure of solace; nor be sure that men of diverse kinds and diverse views can live peaceably together in a time of troubles.

But we can all remind ourselves that the richness of this country was not born in the resources of the earth, though they be plentiful, but in the men that took its measure. For that reminder is everywhere—in the cities, towns, farms, roads, factories, homes, hospitals, schools that spread everywhere over that wilderness.

We can remind ourselves that for all our social discord we yet remain the longest enduring society of free men governing themselves without benefit of kings or dictators. Being so, we are the marvel and the mystery of the world, for that enduring liberty is no less a blessing than the abundance of the earth.

And we might remind ourselves also, that if those men setting out from Delftshaven had been daunted by the troubles they saw around them, then we could not this autumn be thankful for a fair land.

Wamsutta

— 1970 —

Frank B. James, a Wampanoag, was invited to speak at a dinner in Plymouth in 1970 commemorating the three hundred fiftieth anniversary of the landing of the Pilgrims. When the organizers saw a draft of his speech, in which James discussed the fate of American Indians after the arrival of the Europeans, they asked him to revise it. He refused and withdrew from the program. He signed the speech with his Wampanoag name. This is an excerpt from the undelivered speech.

IT IS WITH mixed emotion that I stand here to share my thoughts. This is a time of celebration for you—celebrating an anniversary of a beginning for the white man in America. A time of looking back, of reflection. It is with a heavy heart that I look back upon what happened to my People. Even before the Pilgrims landed it was common practice for ex-

plorers to capture Indians, take them to Europe and sell them as slaves for 220 shillings apiece. The Pilgrims had hardly explored the shores of Cape Cod for four days before they had robbed the graves of my ancestors and stolen their corn and beans....

Massasoit, the great Sachem of the Wampanoag, knew these facts, yet he and his People welcomed and befriended the settlers of the Plymouth Plantation.... This action by Massasoit was perhaps our biggest mistake.

We, the Wampanoag, welcomed you, the white man, with open arms, little knowing that it was the beginning of the end; that before 50 years were to pass, the Wampanoag would no longer be a free people....

Although time has drained our culture, and our language is almost extinct, we the Wampanoags still walk the lands of Massachusetts. We may be fragmented, we may be confused. Many years have passed since we have been a people together. Our lands were invaded. We fought as hard to keep our land as you the whites did to take our land away from us. We were conquered, we became the American prisoners of war in many cases, and wards of the United States Government, until only recently.

Our spirit refuses to die.... What has happened cannot be changed, but today we must work towards a more humane America, a more Indian America, where men and nature once again are important; where the Indian values of honor, truth, and brotherhood prevail. You the white man are celebrating an anniversary. We the Wampanoags will help you celebrate in the concept of a beginning. It was the beginning of a new life for the Pilgrims. Now, 350 years later it is a beginning of a new determination for the original American: the American Indian....

We are determined, and our presence here this evening is living testimony that this is only the beginning of the American Indian, particularly the Wampanoag, to regain the position in this country that is rightfully ours.

Wamsutta
September 10, 1970

The full text of Wamsutta's speech is available on the website of the United American Indians of New England at www.uaine.org.

Linus van Pelt

— 1973 —

In the 1973 holiday special A Charlie Brown Thanksgiving, *the familiar comic strip characters are sitting down to an improvised Thanksgiving dinner of popcorn and toast when Peppermint Patty poses a question. Linus responds.*

PEPPERMINT PATTY: It's Thanksgiving, you know. Before we're served shouldn't we say grace?

LINUS: In the year 1621, the Pilgrims held their first Thanksgiving feast. They invited the great Indian chief Massasoit, who brought ninety of his brave Indians and a great abundance of food. Governor William Bradford and Captain Miles Standish were honored guests. Elder William Brewster, who was a minister, said a prayer that went something like this: "We thank God for our homes and our food and our safety in a new land. We thank God for the opportunity to create a new world for freedom and justice."

PEPPERMINT PATTY: Amen.

Moorhead C. Kennedy Jr.

— 1981 —

Moorhead C. Kennedy Jr. was one of more than sixty American diplomats and citizens taken hostage by Iran shortly before Thanksgiving in November 1979. The Americans were freed on January 20, 1981, the day Ronald Reagan was inaugurated as president of the United States. The former hos-

tage spoke to the New York Times *on the eve of Thanksgiving 1981, the first Thanksgiving after his release.*

I CELEBRATED two Thanksgivings in captivity: The first one we thought we were going to be killed. On the second we were bored out of our minds. I'll be celebrating this one at home with my wife, three boys and my parents. It will be the first Thanksgiving in which I've ever experienced the need to be thankful. Before that it was just a day off, nice but with no special significance. We'll be eating the conventional meal, which is amusing in a way. When we were in captivity they fed us with turkeys stolen from the embassy freezer. Half-done bloody turkey was a hostage staple and one we will never forget.

From Moira Hodgson, "Special Holiday Touch by Special People," New York Times, *November 18, 1981.*

George W. Bush
— 2 0 0 3 —

President George W. Bush paid a surprise visit to Iraq on Thanksgiving Day 2003, an event he called "the most thrilling trip of my presidency." He writes about it in his memoir, Decision Points *(Crown, 2010).*

WAITING FOR ME at the airport were Jerry Bremer and General Ricardo Sanchez, the senior ground commander in Iraq. "Welcome to Iraq," Jerry said. We went to the mess hall, where six

hundred troops had gathered for a Thanksgiving meal. Jerry was supposed to be the guest of honor. He told the troops he had a holiday message from the president. "Let's see if we've got anybody more senior here…," he said.

That was my cue. I walked out from behind a curtain and onto the stage of the packed hall. Many of the stunned troops hesitated for a split second, then let out deafening whoops and hooahs. Some had tears running down their faces. I was swept up by the emotion. These were the souls who just eight months earlier had liberated Iraq on my orders. Many had seen combat. Some had seen friends perish. I took a deep breath and said, "I bring a message on behalf of America. We thank you for your service, we're proud of you, and America stands solidly behind you."

Adam Lee

— 2 0 0 6 —

Adam Lee, who blogs on atheism, wrote this non-prayer, titled "An Atheist Benediction," to be spoken before Thanksgiving dinner.

AS WE COME TOGETHER to share this meal, let us first remember how it came to us and be thankful to the people who made it possible.

This food was born from the bounty of the Earth, in warm sunlight, rich earth and cool rain.

May it nourish us, in body and mind, and provide us with the things that are good for living.

We are grateful to those who cultivated it, those who harvested it, those who brought it to us, and those who prepared it.

May its consumption bring about the pleasures of friendship, love and good company.

And as we partake of this food in each other's company, as what was once separate from all of us becomes part of each of us, may we also remember what we have in common and what brings us all together.

May this sharing of food foster peace and understanding among us, may it bring us to the recognition that we depend on each other for all the good we can ever hope to receive, and that all the good we can hope to accomplish rests in helping others in turn.

May it remind us that as we reach out to others to brighten their lives so are our lives brightened in turn.

Used with the permission of Adam Lee, www.patheos.com/blogs/daylightatheism.

Billy Graham

— 2013 —

The evangelist Billy Graham responded on his website, www.billygraham. org, to a question from a foreign student, who asked: "What is the meaning of the holiday you call 'Thanksgiving'? Does it have something to do with Christianity?"

THANK YOU for your question, and welcome to our country! I hope your letter will encourage us to make friends with students who come here from other nations. The Bible (the source of our Christian faith) says, "The foreigner residing among you must be treated as your native-born. Love them as yourself" (Leviticus 19:34).

Some of our holidays are directly related to the Christian faith, such as Christmas (commemorating the birth of Jesus) and Easter (celebrating the resurrection of Jesus from the dead). Others are secular, remembering events in our nation's history (such as July 4, marking the beginning of our independence).

Thanksgiving is somewhat in between, and is set aside each year by Presidential decree as a time to be thankful for our blessings as a nation. Not everyone in America is religious or Christian (as you'll discover), but those of us who are see Thanksgiving especially as a day to thank God for His goodness to us. The Bible says, "Give thanks to the Lord, for he is good; his love endures forever" (Psalm 107:1).

As we observe Thanksgiving next week, may it be a time of reflection for each of us, recalling the blessings we enjoy every day—blessings that come from God's gracious hand. And may it cause each of us (including you) to turn in faith to the living God and discover His great love for us. God has blessed us in many ways—but most of all by sending Jesus Christ into the world for our salvation.

Thanksgiving

Recipes

AND

Bills of Fare

Pompkin Pudding & Tarts
— 1796 —

Amelia Simmons's American Cookery *(1796) was the first cookbook published in the United States, and the first to include recipes for dishes using ingredients indigenous to North America.* American Cookery *includes several recipes for pumpkin pie or, as Simmons calls it, pumpkin "pudding." She clearly is describing what we would call a pie, as the recipe calls for the use of a "paste" or pie crust. Simmons provides nine numbered recipes for "pastes" elsewhere in the book.*

POMPKIN PUDDING

No. 1. One quart stewed and strained (pumpkin), 3 pints cream, 9 beaten eggs, sugar, mace, nutmeg and ginger, laid into paste No. 7 or 3 and with a dough spur,* cross and chequer it, and baked in dishes three quarters of an hour.

No. 2. One quart of milk, 1 pint pumpkin, 4 eggs, molasses, allspice and ginger in a crust, bake 1 hour.

* *A pastry wheel*

American Cookery *also contains recipes for apple and cranberry tarts.*

APPLE TARTS

Stew and strain the apples, add cinnamon, rosewater, wine and sugar to your taste, lay in paste No. 1 and bake gently.

CRANBERRIES TART

Stewed, strained and sweetened, put into paste No. 9, and bake gently.

Cranberry Pie

— 1829 —

Lydia Maria Child's The Frugal Housewife *was published in 1829 and quickly became what food historian Janice Bluestein Longone has called "the standard American cookbook of its time." It went through thirty-three printings over the next quarter century. Child was a prolific writer and one of the nineteenth century's best-known abolitionists. She also wrote "The New-England Boy's Song about Thanksgiving Day," a poem whose better-known, unofficial title is taken from its first line, "Over the river, and through the wood." Here is her recipe for cranberry pie.*

CRANBERRY PIE

Cranberry pies need very little spice. A little nutmeg, or cinnamon, improves them. They need a great deal of sweetening. It is well to stew the sweetening with them; at least a part of it. It is easy to add, if you find them too sour for your taste. When cranberries are strained, and added to about their own weight in sugar, they make very delicious tarts. No upper crust.

Cranberry Sauce & Roast Turkey

— 1857 —

Sarah Josepha Hale published several cookbooks during her editorship of
Godey's Lady's Book. *One, published in 1857 by T. B. Peterson & Brothers
of Philadelphia, carries the descriptive title:* Mrs. Hale's New Cook Book:
A Practical System for Private Families in Town and Country; with
Directions for Carving, and Arranging the Table for Parties, Etc.;
also, Preparations of Food for Invalids and for Children. *In the preface,
Mrs. Hale explains that "because the Republic is made up from the people of
all lands," the book contains "the best receipts from the Domestic Economy
of the different nations of the Old World." The preface notes, too, that she
has included many fish and vegetable recipes in deference to the "large and
increasing class of persons in our country who abstain from flesh meats during
Lent"—i.e. Roman Catholic immigrants. But her focus is on American recipes, she says, which she has collected from ladies "famed for their excellent
housekeeping, with large collections of original receipts, which those ladies
have tested in their own families."*

CRANBERRY SAUCE

This sauce is very simply made. A quart of cranberries are washed
and stewed with sufficient water to cover them; when they burst

mix with them a pound of brown sugar and
stir them well. Before you remove them
from the fire, all the berries should have
burst. When cold they will be jellied, and
if thrown into a form while warm, will turn
out whole.

Or if you prefer:

To Stew Cranberries

To a pound of Cranberries allow a pound of sugar; dissolve the sugar in a very little water, boil it for ten minutes, and skim it well. Have the cranberries well washed, put them with the sugar and boil them slowly till they are quite soft, and of a fine color.

Mrs. Hale included several recipes for turkey, including boiled turkey, roast turkey, deviled turkey, and a recommendation to use turkey in pie.

To Roast a Turkey

Prepare a stuffing of pork sausage meat, one beaten egg, and a few crumbs of bread; or, if sausages are to be served with the turkey, stuffing as for fillet of veal. In either, a little shred shalot [*sic*] is an improvement. Stuff the bird under the breast; dredge it with flour, and put it down to a clear brisk fire; at a moderate distance the first half-hour, but afterwards nearer. Baste with butter; and when the turkey is plumped up, and the steam draws towards the fire, it will be nearly done; then dredge it lightly with flour, and baste it with a little more  butter, first melted in the basting-ladle. Serve with gravy in the dish, and bread sauces in a tureen. It may be garnished with sausages, or with fried forcemeat, if veal-stuffing be used. Sometimes the gizzard and liver are dipped into the yolk of an egg, sprinkled with salt and cayenne, and then put under the pinion, before the bird is put to the fire. Chestnuts, stewed in gravy, are likewise eaten with turkey.

A very large turkey will require three hours' roasting; one of eight or ten pounds, two hours; and a small one, an hour and a half.

Roasted chestnuts, grated or sliced, and green truffles, sliced, are excellent additions to the stuffing for turkeys.

Charles Dickens ate roast turkey with truffles when he toured the United States in 1842.

Civil War Dinner for Wounded Soldiers

— 1864 —

In a page-one story on the day after Thanksgiving 1864, the Evening Star *of Washington, D.C. reported on the special Thanksgiving Day dinners that had been served at local hospitals for wounded and sick soldiers. At Armory Square Hospital, five hundred fifty patients attended the afternoon dinner, along with a large detachment of men from the Veteran Reserve Corps who had been assigned to the hospital as nurses or guards. The* Evening Star *described the large hall where the dinner took place. American flags were on display at both ends of the room, and along one wall was a banner that said "National Thanksgiving." 1864 was the year of Lincoln's second proclamation for a national Thanksgiving. Here is the menu.*

Meats
Roast beef, roast veal, boiled ham

Poultry
Roast turkey, roast goose, chicken pie

Confectionery
Cranberry sauce, cranberry tart, apple pie, mixed cakes, jellies

Sundries
Smoked beef, bologna sausage, bread, butter,
celery, oyster stew, oysters raw, cheese, crackers, ice cream

Fish
Baked rock fish, boiled codfish

Vegetables
Sweet potatoes, Irish potatoes, kale slaw,
pickled cucumbers, pickled beets

Fruits
Apples, almonds, raisins, figs

Coffee, tea, cocoa

Old-Fashioned Pumpkin Pie
— 1893 —

From the New York Evening World, *November 30, 1893, a recipe for pumpkin pie:*

FOR EACH PIE allow one and a half cupfuls of stewed and sifted pumpkins, one cupful of boiling milk, half a cupful of brown sugar, half a teaspoonful of salt, one-half a saltspoonful* of cinnamon, one half a saltspoonful of ginger, and two eggs. Line a deep pie-plate with good paste, put on a rim, and fill with the pumpkin.

* *A saltspoon is equivalent to ¼ teaspoon.*

Fannie Farmer's Thanksgiving Dinner
— 1896 —

Fannie Merritt Farmer's Boston Cooking-School Cookbook *is one of the best-selling cookbooks in the United States. Since it was first published in 1896, it has gone through many printings. Part of its popularity was due to the fact that unlike most cookbooks of the day its recipes were concise and easy to follow. Miss Farmer used standardized measurements—the precise "one teaspoon," for example, rather than vague instructions such as "a pinch" or "a handful." Her elaborate menu for Thanksgiving dinner sounds like it could have fed the entire faculty and student body of the Boston Cooking-School.*

Oyster Soup – Crisp Crackers

Celery – Salted Almonds

Roast Turkey, Cranberry Jelly

Mashed Potatoes – Onions in Cream

Chicken Pie

Fruit Pudding, Sterling Sauce*

Mince, Apple, and Squash Pie

Neapolitan Ice Cream – Fancy Cakes

Fruit – Nuts and Raisins – Bonbons

Crackers – Cheese – Cafe Noir

* *Sterling Sauce is a vanilla sauce for puddings and other desserts.*

Succotash is the traditional dish at Forefathers Day dinners, a custom that originated at the first Forefathers Day gathering in 1769. There are numerous recipes for succotash, the easiest of which—prep time: two minutes—is to open a can of corn and a can of lima beans and heat them up together in a pot on top of the stove. Authentic succotash takes far longer to prepare. A classic recipe appeared in 1915 in the proceedings of the Colonial Society of Massachusetts:

Boil two fowls in a large kettle of water. At the same time boil in another kettle one-half pound of lean pork and two quarts of common white beans, until like soup. When the fowls are boiled, skim off the fat and add a small piece of corned beef, one-half of a turnip sliced and cut small, and five or six potatoes sliced thin.

When cooked tender, take out the fowls and keep them in the oven with the pork. The soup of beans and pork should be added to the water the fowls and beef were boiled in. Add salt and pepper. Four quarts of hulled corn having been boiled soft are added to the soup. Before serving, add the meat of one fowl. The second fowl should be served separately, as also the corned beef and pork.

Any recipe that begins "Boil two fowls" is unlikely to appeal to modern-day cooks, and succotash has mostly fallen out of culinary fashion today. Even so, references to it still pop up, especially around Thanksgiving, when it sometimes puts in an appearance on holiday menus.

World War I Thanksgiving Dinner

— 1918 —

The armistice ending World War I was signed on November 11, 1918. On November 23, the Topeka Daily State Journal *in Kansas published a lengthy article by Frederic J. Haskin, a nationally syndicated columnist, under the headline "Thanksgiving Dinner for the United States." Haskin warned that turkeys would be expensive and rather scarce that year, since the War Department had bought so many turkeys to send to the one and a half million American soldiers stationed in Europe. He urged readers to consider buying goose, duck, or chicken instead of the "national bird." Among the recipes he included at the end of his article is this one for a rice-based stuffing.*

ORIENTAL STUFFING

½ tablespoon fat, 1 cup rice, ½ cup raisins, ½ cup nuts (use locally grown nuts), liver of the fowl. Salt and pepper to taste. Cook the rice, and mix well the seedless raisins, the nuts and the chopped liver of the turkey together with the fat, season to taste, stuff the fowl with it, and proceed with the roasting.

Turkey, Chicken, or Macaroni?

— 1919 —

In its November 1919 issue, American Cookery *magazine published several menus for Thanksgiving dinner. Its recommended menu for an "old-fashioned" New England–style Thanksgiving dinner included roast turkey with cranberry sauce. But it also published three menus for dinners without turkey, presumably for those who could not afford it. One menu substituted roast pork tenderloin with spiced grape jelly. Another called for roast chicken with stuffing and currant jelly. The third, for "kitchenette housekeeping," recommended the substitution of macaroni and chicken pudding for the traditional roast turkey. Here is the menu for an old-fashioned New England Thanksgiving dinner.*

Oyster Cocktail or Grapefruit Consommé

Roast Turkey, Cranberry Sauce

Mashed Potato – Mashed Turnips

Boiled Onions – Creamed Cauliflower

Olives – Celery – Salted Almonds

Homemade Relishes

Pineapple Sherbet

Pumpkin Pie – Mince Pie

Apples – Raisins – Nuts

Sweet Cider – Coffee

Thanksgiving Dinner at the White House

— 1942 —

On Thanksgiving Day 1942, Franklin Roosevelt read his first wartime Thanksgiving proclamation over the radio. The president then led the nation in a prayer for victory. After the radio broadcast, he and First Lady Elea-nor Roosevelt had dinner at the White House rather than in Warm Springs, Georgia, where they often spent the holiday. This was the menu.

Clam Cocktail

Clear Soup

Roast Turkey with Chestnut Stuffing and Cranberry Sauce

Spanish Corn – Small Sausages and Beans – Sweet Potato Cones

 Grapefruit Salad

Pumpkin Pie – Cheese – Ice Cream

Coffee

A GI Thanksgiving

— 1944 —

The War Department published Army Recipes, a.k.a. Technical Manual TM10-4121, *on August 15, 1944. It was a year before World War II ended, and the United States had approximately fifteen million men and women under arms at the time. The book's Introduction advises the Army cook that he "needs more than recipes. He needs practice, imagination and, above all, a desire to*

please those who eat the food he prepares. The soldier who develops these quali-
ties and follows the recipes provided for him soon becomes a skillful cook."

No 629.
BAKED SWEET POTATOES WITH APPLES AND MARSHMALLOWS
Yield: 100 servings, approximately ½ cup each

Potatoes, sweet—32 pounds

Salt—2½ ounces (5 mess kit spoons)

Water, boiling

Sugar, brown—2½ pounds (2 no. 56 dippers)

Apples, tart, sliced—8 pounds (8 no. 56 dippers)

Butter—6 ounces (¼ mess kit cup)

1. Wash sweet potatoes; pare and cut into crosswise slices ¼ inch thick.

2. Cover sweet potatoes with boiling salted water. Cover and heat to boiling point; reduce heat and simmer until tender. Drain.

3. Arrange potato slices overlapping one another in well greased baking pans.

4. Sprinkle with salt and ½ the sugar.

5. Cover potato slices with a layer of sliced apples.

6. Sprinkle apples with remaining sugar. Place pieces of butter on top of apples.

7. Bake in moderate oven (350° F.) until apples are tender.

Add 1 pound marshmallows to recipe for baked sweet potatoes and apples. Cut marshmallows into quarters and place on top of layers of sweet potatoes and apples in baking pans.

Oysters for Thanksgiving

— 1954 —

Shortly before Thanksgiving in 1954, the Interior Department issued a press release titled "Oysters—A Thanksgiving Tradition." The Pilgrims and Indians ate oysters at the First Thanksgiving, it said, and modern-day families can follow in their footsteps. This recipe for oyster stuffing was among several recipes provided by the home economists of the department's Fish and Wildlife Service.

OYSTER STUFFING

1 pint oysters

½ cup chopped celery

½ cup chopped onion

¼ cup butter

4 cups day-old bread cubes

1 tablespoon chopped parsley

1 teaspoon salt

Dash poultry seasoning

Dash pepper

Drain oysters, saving liquor, and chop. Cook celery and onion in butter until tender. Combine oysters, cooked vegetables, bread cubes, and seasonings, and mix thoroughly. If stuffing seems dry, moisten with oyster liquor. Makes enough for a 4-pound chicken.

OYSTER STUFFING FOR TURKEY

For 10–15 lb. turkey: 3 times above recipe

For 16–20 lb. turkey: 4 times above recipe

For 21–25 lb. turkey: 5 times above recipe

Indian Pudding

Indian pudding is a classic New England dessert that still appears on regional menus, most famously at Durgin-Park Restaurant at Faneuil Hall in Boston. Despite its name, the dish originated not with Native Americans but with colonial cooks, who referred to anything that contained cornmeal as "Indian." Amelia Simmons *included three recipes for Indian pudding in* American Cookery. *This recipe comes from Durgin-Park, which has been serving Indian pudding since the eighteenth century.*

INDIAN PUDDING

1½ cups milk plus another 1½ cups milk

¼ cup black molasses

2 tablespoons sugar

2 tablespoons butter

¼ teaspoon salt

⅛ teaspoon baking powder

1 egg

½ cup yellow cornmeal

Preheat the oven to 450 F. In a bowl mix 1½ cups of the milk with the molasses, sugar, butter, salt, baking powder, egg and cornmeal. Pour the mixture into a stone crock that has been well greased and bake until it boils. Heat and stir in the remaining 1½ cups milk. Lower the oven temperature to 300 F and bake for 5 to 7 hours. Serve warm with whipped cream or vanilla ice cream.

Makes 4 to 6 servings.

This recipe is courtesy of Durgin-Park Restaurant.

Acknowledgments

The idea for this book was born in the aftermath of the terrorist attacks of September 11, 2001. I was in downtown Manhattan that morning and saw the burning towers of the World Trade Center collapse into dust, killing more than three thousand innocent people. A few weeks later I began to read *Of Plymouth Plantation*, William Bradford's firsthand account of the Pilgrims' journey to America and their founding of a new community. Bradford's narrative was a revelation. I encountered people who grappled four centuries ago with issues that 9/11 had brought to the fore—issues of religious freedom, self-defense, the rule of law. At the heart of the Pilgrims' story was a theme that I, like many others, had recently been pondering: what it means to be American.

With November approaching, I skipped ahead to Bradford's description of the event that has come to be known as the First Thanksgiving, when the Pilgrims, having endured great suffering the previous winter, paused to give thanks for their survival and their renewed blessings. In just a few words, Bradford sketched a scene remarkably similar to the holiday that Americans still celebrate. I wanted to learn more about this little kernel of history and how it grew into a cherished national tradition.

Many people helped me fill out the story. Short portions of this book first appeared as op-eds in the *Wall Street Journal*, whose skillful editors improved them.

I am indebted to all the librarians who assisted me. At the top of the list is my stepdaughter, Jacqueline David, a careful, precise researcher who delved into years of *Godey's Lady's Book* to find articles related to Thanksgiving. She also compiled a list of movies and TV shows set around the holiday. She has my deep appreciation. I am grateful to Valerie Berlin of the Licia & Mason Beekley Community Library in New Hartford, Connecticut, for tracking down books of interest, and to Christina Kasman, librarian of the Yale Club of New York, for offering research tips. Librarians at the Connecticut State Library and the University of Texas also proved helpful.

I thank James Bologna, who uncovered information on obscure bits of the holiday's history. He is expert at online research and has excellent judgment about what constitutes a good story.

There aren't many books about Thanksgiving for readers over the age of eight, but there are a few that I often turned to: *The Fast and Thanksgiving Days of New England* by William DeLoss Love (1895); *Thanksgiving: An American Holiday, an American History* by Diana Karter Appelbaum (1984); and *Thanksgiving: The Biography of an American Holiday* by James W. Baker (2009).

The websites of Pilgrim Hall Museum and Plimoth Plantation are indispensable for learning about Thanksgiving, the Pilgrims, and the Wampanoag. I am very grateful to Patrick Browne, former executive director of Pilgrim Hall, and Stephen O'Neill, former associate director and curator, for their assistance. Plimoth Plantation's John Kemp provided a wealth of information about Bradford, Pastor John Robinson, and the Pilgrims' style of prayer. Mike Coleman gave me a fascinating tour of the Colony Club's historic facility in downtown Plymouth and entertained me with club lore.

I am grateful to John Holtzapple, director of the James K. Polk Home and Museum in Columbia, Tennessee, for sharing his research on President and Mrs. Polk, who may unwittingly have hosted the first Thanksgiving dinner at the White House. Al Borrego, president of the San Elizario Genealogical Society, provided an overview of the first Thanksgiving commemorations in San Elizario, Texas. Graham Woodlief, president of the Virginia Thanksgiving Festival and a descendant of Captain John Woodlief, the leader of the early settlement at Berkeley Plantation, told me about Thanksgiving in Virginia and gave me copies of historical documents.

I appreciate the assistance of Paul Shipman and his colleagues at the Connecticut Food Bank in Wallingford, where I spent a day observing their impressive operation. I also thank Henry Timms, executive director of the 92nd Street Y in New York City, for explaining how Giving Tuesday got started.

One of the pleasures of writing a book about Americans' favorite holiday is that friends and acquaintances wanted to relate favorite anecdotes or point me to little-known pieces of history. Marshall Miller told me about Berkeley, Virginia. Tony Lee encouraged me to research Thanksgiving football. Desislava Taliokova described Black Friday in Bulgaria. Elizabeth Lockwood Gunnell offered thoughts on the challenges of family dynamics at the holiday. Steve Greene told me about football in the nineteenth century. Bill Ducci, a veteran deer hunter in New England, calculated how many meals could come from the five white-tail deer the Wampanoag brought to the feast in 1621. David Steinman shared helpful information about politically correct takes on Thanksgiving in the academy. Amity Shlaes tracked down the remarks of Calvin Coolidge on the tercentennial of the *Mayflower*'s arrival. Conversations with William J. Haynes and Elizabeth Chandler helped me structure the "Readings for Thanksgiving Day."

I am grateful for the encouragement of Kenneth R. Weinstein, president and CEO of the Hudson Institute, of which I am a senior fellow, and Robert Dilenschneider, founder of the Dilenschneider Group, who circulates a marvelous fact sheet on the holiday every November. I thank Karen Kelly for helpful advice and an introduction to Newcomers High School. I am deeply grateful to my friend Alice Volpe for her early support on this project.

Several people read portions of the manuscript and made good suggestions. Robert Asahina read an early draft of sections of the book and offered helpful ideas for the structure of the whole. My stepson Zachary David, a gifted writer whose pen name is Zachary Watterson, advised me on the opening chapters. Gail Buyske, whom I first met on

Thanksgiving Day in Hong Kong in the early 1980s, cast a literary eye on "Readings for Thanksgiving Day." George Melloan, a former colleague at the *Wall Street Journal* and author of *When the New Deal Comes to Town*, provided historical context on FDR and the Depression. Kay Ellen Consolver gave a careful reading to "Recipes and Bills of Fare."

My agents, Glen Hartley and Lynn Chu, were enthusiastic from the start, even though some in the publishing world informed us that "Thanksgiving is not a book-buying holiday." Glen and Lynn found the ideal publisher in Encounter Books, home of an extraordinary team of accomplished and committed professionals. I thank Roger Kimball, Nola Tully, Heather Ohle, Katherine Wong, Sam Schneider, and Lauren Miklos. My editor, Carol Staswick, is a gem. *Thanksgiving* is a better book thanks to Carol's editorial improvements.

I had the very good fortune to work with Katherine Messenger, a talented designer and illustrator. Early in the production process, Heather Ohle, Encounter's creative director of production, told me she had found the perfect artist for *Thanksgiving*. She was right. I thank Katherine for her imaginative and intelligent drawings, which capture the spirit of the book. Heather and Katherine were a pleasure to work with, and I learned a lot from them. I thank them for including me, a word person, in their artistic process.

This book is dedicated to my sisters, Holly Whiting and Robin Koves, and to the memory of our parents, William C. Kirkpatrick Jr. and Virginia Reyburn Kirkpatrick. Holly, Robin, and I share many happy memories of Thanksgiving when we were growing up in Buffalo. We may not have gone "over the river and through the woods" to grandmother's house, but we often made our way through "white and drifted snow."

My deepest appreciation goes to my husband, Jack David. I am grateful for his encouragement and enthusiastic support. He is also a superb editor, and *Thanksgiving* benefited enormously from his input. Finally, his talents extend to roasting the turkey that anchors our Thanksgiving dinner every year. For all this, and more, I thank him.

MELANIE KIRKPATRICK
July 2016

NOTES

Introduction: Newcomers

1. Samuel Eliot Morison, *The Pilgrim Fathers: Their Significance in History* (Concord, N.H.: Society of Mayflower Descendants in the State of New Hampshire, 1937), 6, as quoted in James W. Baker, *Thanksgiving: The Biography of an American Holiday* (Hanover: University of New Hampshire Press, 2009), 113.

Chapter One: The First Thanksgiving

1. Interview with Patrick Browne, executive director, Pilgrim Hall Museum, December 2013.

2. William Bradford, *Of Plymouth Plantation, 1620–1647*, ed. Samuel Eliot Morison (New York: Knopf, 2000), 90.

3. Edward Winslow, "A Letter Sent from New England to a Friend," *Mourt's Relation*, ed. Dwight B. Heath (1623; Bedford, Mass.: Applewood Books, 1963), 82.

4. William DeLoss Love, *The Fast and Thanksgiving Days of New England* (Boston: Houghton, Mifflin & Co., 1895), 244.

5. Ibid., 69.

6. John Robinson, *The Works of John Robinson, Pastor of the Pilgrim Fathers*, ed. Robert Ashton (London: John Snow, 1851), vol. 1, 196.

7. "The 53 Pilgrims at the First Thanksgiving," Pilgrim Hall Museum, http://www.pilgrimhallmuseum.org.

8. Bradford, *Of Plymouth Plantation*, 81.

9. Ibid., 131–32.

10. Love, *The Fast and Thanksgiving Days of New England,* 167.

11. Ibid., 162–76.

12. Ibid., 168–69.

13. *The Public Records of the Colony of Connecticut Prior to the Union with New Haven Colony* (Hartford: Brown & Parsons, 1850), 33.

14. This opinion is attributed to a "Mr. Torrey" in a debate that took place in 1690 in the Governor's Council of the Massachusetts Bay Colony, as described by Judge Samuel Sewall in his diary. See Diana Karter Appelbaum, *Thanksgiving: An American Holiday, an American History* (New York: Facts on File, 1984), 31–32.

15. Charles Francis Adams, *Three Episodes of Massachusetts History,* 2nd ed. (Boston: Houghton, Mifflin & Co., 1892), vol. 2, 625–26.

16. *Reports of Cases Argued and Determined in the Supreme Court of Errors of the State of Connecticut,* 2nd ed. (New York: Banks, Gould & Co., 1849), 49–54.

17. Appelbaum, *Thanksgiving: An American Holiday,* 36.

18. "Thanksgiving Day," Letter to the Editor, *Norwich Weekly Register,* as reprinted in the *Connecticut Courant,* December 10, 1792.

19. "Thanksgiving: How the Day Was Passed in Boston," *Boston Daily Globe,* November 28, 1873.

20. "Thanksgiving Day," *Educational Research Bulletin* 5:18 (December 1, 1926), 382–83.

21. Robert D. Putnam and David E. Campbell, *American Grace: How Religion Divides and Unites Us* (New York: Simon & Schuster, 2010), 10.

22. Ayn Rand, "Cashing In on Hunger," *Ayn Rand Letter* 3:23 (August 12, 1974).

23. Edward Bleier, *The Thanksgiving Ceremony: New Traditions for America's Family Feast* (New York: Crown, 2003).

Chapter 2: Before the Pilgrims

1. Suzanne Gamboa, "Thanksgiving Pilgrimage: New Englanders Go to El Paso to Press Claim on Holiday," *Dallas Morning News,* April 25, 1992.

2. Gaspar Pérez de Villagrá, *Historica de la Nueva México, 1610: A Critical and Annotated Spanish/English Edition,* ed. Alfred Rodríguez, Joseph P.

Sánchez, and Miguel Encinias (Albuquerque: University of New Mexico Press, 1992).

3. Ibid., 126.

4. Ibid.

5. Ibid., 130.

6. "Proclamation by the Governor of Texas," Official Memorandum, State of Texas, Office of the Governor, April 18, 1991.

7. Al Borrego, president of the San Elizario Genealogical and Historical Society, in conversation with the author, March 2014.

8. Michael V. Gannon, *The Cross in the Sand* (Gainesville: University Presses of Florida, 1965), 1–2.

9. Ibid., 24–26.

10. H. Graham Woodlief, "History of the First Thanksgiving," on the website of the Virginia Thanksgiving Festival, http:virginiathanksgivingfestival.com; and Matt Blitz, "The First Thanksgiving Took Place in Virginia, Not Massachusetts," *Washingtonian*, November 18, 2015.

11. Lyon G. Tyler, "First Thanksgiving in America Was Decreed for Town of Berkeley on James," *Richmond News Leader*, April 3, 1931.

12. "President Concedes: Virginia Receives Thanksgiving Credit," *Richmond News Leader*, November 5, 1963.

13. "President Bush Offers Thanksgiving Greetings," White House press release, November 19, 2007.

14. "If You Want to Be Historically Accurate This Holiday, Serve Alligator," Jacksonville Historical Society, http://www.jaxhistory.org/timucua_first_thanksgiving/.

15. Myron Beckenstein, "Maine's Lost Colony," *Smithsonian*, February 2004.

16. Rear-Admiral Richard Collinson, *The Three Voyages of Martin Frobisher, in Search of a Passage to Cathaia and India by the North-West, A.D. 1576–8* (London: Hakluyt Society, 1867; New York: Burt Franklin, [1963]), 251–52.

17. Edward Winslow, *Good Newes from New England: A True Relation of Things Very Remarkable at the Plantation of Plimoth in New England* (1624; Bedford, Mass.: Applewood Books, 1998), 38–39.

Chapter 3: America Discovers the Pilgrims

1. William Bradford, *Of Plymouth Plantation, 1620–1647*, ed. Samuel Eliot Morison (New York: Knopf, 2000), 47.

2. Bill Bryson, *Made in America: An Informal History of the English Language in the United States* (New York: HarperCollins, 2015), 2.

3. Bradford, *Of Plymouth Plantation*, 72.

4. The history of the Old Colony Club and descriptions of the early Forefathers Day celebrations are found in James Thacher, *History of the Town of Plymouth, from Its First Settlement in 1620 to the Present Time*, 2nd ed. (Boston: Marsh, Capen & Lyon, 1835), 180–96.

5. Ibid.

6. Mary J. Lincoln, *Mrs. Lincoln's New England Cookbook* (1883; Bedford, Mass.: Applewood Books, 2008), 284.

7. Forefathers Day Dinner in Plymouth, Massachusetts, December 21, 2013.

8. Thacher, *History of the Town of Plymouth*, 196.

9. "Celebration of the Landing of the Pilgrim Fathers in America," *Oriental Herald*, vol. 6, June–September 1825 (London: Sandford Arnot, 1825), 81–86.

10. J. S. Buckingham, *America, Historical, Statistic, and Descriptive* (New York: Harper & Brothers, 1841), vol. 2, 456–60.

11. John Seelye, *Memory's Nation: The Place of Plymouth Rock* (Chapel Hill: University of North Carolina Press, 1998), 269.

12. Daniel Webster, *A Discourse, Delivered at Plymouth, December 23, 1820, in Commemoration of the First Settlement of New-England* (Boston: Wells & Lilly, 1821), 11.

13. Ibid., 30.

14. Ibid., 93.

15. James W. Baker, *Thanksgiving: The Biography of an American Holiday* (Durham, N.H.: University of New Hampshire Press, 2009), 12–13.

16. Alexander Young, *Chronicles of the Pilgrim Fathers* (Boston: Charles C. Little & James Brown, 1841), 231, n.3.

17. Bradford's manuscript was returned to Massachusetts in 1897.

18. Baker, *Thanksgiving: The Biography of an American Holiday*, 13.

Chapter 4: George Washington Sets the Stage

1. The first Congress's debate on Thanksgiving in September 1789 is recorded in the *Annals of Congress* at the Library of Congress's website, https://memory.loc.gov/ammem/amlaw/lwac.html.

2. "Thanksgiving Proclamation," October 3, 1789, *The Papers of George Washington*, Digital Edition, ed. Theodore J. Crackel et al. (Charlottesville: University of Virginia Press, Rotunda, 2007–).

3. Ibid.

4. Ibid.

5. George Washington to Catherine Macaulay Graham, January 9, 1790, TeachingAmericanHistory.org, http://teachingamericanhistory.org/library/document/letter-to-catherine-macaulay-graham/.

6. Thomas Jefferson to Samuel Miller, January 23, 1808, Founders Online, National Archives, http://founders.archives.gov/documents/Jefferson/99-01-02-7257.

7. I consulted several sources for the story of the Charleston Jews' boycott of Thanksgiving 1844, among them: "The Israelites of South Carolina," *The Occidental and American Jewish Advocate*, January 1845; Drew Gilpin Faust, *James Henry Hammond and the Old South: A Design for Mastery* (Baton Rouge: LSU Press, 1985); and Robert N. Rosen, *The Jewish Confederates* (Columbia: University of South Carolina Press, 2000).

Chapter 5: Thanksgiving's Godmother

1. Ruth E. Finley, *The Lady of Godey's* (Philadelphia: J. B. Lippincott Co., 1931), 22.

2. Patricia Okker, *Our Sister Editors: Sarah J. Hale and the Tradition of Nineteenth-Century American Women Editors* (Athens: University of Georgia Press, 1995), 1–2.

3. Finley, *The Lady of Godey's*, 29.

4. Sarah Josepha Buell Hale, ed., *The Ladies' Wreath: A Selection from the Female Poetic Writers of England and America* (Boston: Marsh, Capen & Lyon, 1837), 386–87.

5. Okker, *Our Sister Editors*, 1–2.

6. Sarah Josepha Hale, *Northwood; or, Life North and South: Showing the True Character of Both*, 2nd ed. (New York: H. Long & Brother, 1852).

7. Zachary Taylor's letter, dated November 6, 1849, was reprinted in *The Republic* (Washington, D.C.) on November 19, 1849, under the heading, "Letter from the President."

8. John Holtzapple, director of the President James K. Polk House and Museum, in correspondence with the author, November 2015.

9. Barton H. Wise, *The Life of Henry A. Wise of Virginia, 1806–1876* (New York: The Macmillan Co., 1899), 214–15.

10. Sarah Josepha Hale, "The National Thanksgiving," *Godey's Lady's Book*, November 1857.

11. Sarah Josepha Hale, "Our Thanksgiving Union," *Godey's Lady's Book*, November 1859.

12. Sarah Josepha Hale, "Thanksgiving: The New National Holiday," *Godey's Lady's Book*, September 1860.

13. "Thanksgiving Day," *Evening Star* (Washington, D.C.), November 25, 1864.

14. Sarah Josepha Hale as quoted in Ella Rodman Church, "Representative Women of Our Own and Other Lands: Life of Sarah Josepha Hale," *Godey's Lady's Book*, July 1879, 70.

15. Ibid.

Chapter 6: The Turkey Bowl

1. Diana Karter Appelbaum, *Thanksgiving: An American Holiday, an American History* (New York: Facts on File, 1984), 163–65.

2. Robert C. Kennedy on Thomas Nast's "Uncle Sam's Thanksgiving Dinner" (originally published in *Harper's Weekly*, November 22, 1869), essay on the HarpWeek "Cartoon of the Day" for November 22 at http://www.harpweek.com.

3. Appelbaum, *Thanksgiving: An American Holiday*, 167.

4. "Origin of Thanksgiving Day," *Highland Recorder* (Monterey, Highland County, Virginia), November 23, 1900.

5. Walter Camp, "Football in America: A Sketch of Our Most Popular

Autumn Sport," *Frank Leslie's Popular Monthly* 47 (November 1898), 56.

6. Melvin I. Smith, *Evolvements of Early American Foot Ball: Through the 1890/91 Season* (Bloomington, Ind.: AuthorHouse, 2008), 3.

7. Kevin Paul Dupont, "Games Pilgrims Play," *Boston Globe*, November 21, 2010.

8. Richard Harding Davis, "The Thanksgiving-Day Game," *Harper's Weekly*, December 9, 1893.

9. Ibid.

10. Ibid.

11. Ibid.

12. Ibid.

13. "Princeton's Great Victory: Its Striped Champions Defeat the Boys in Blue in One of the Greatest of Games," *New York Herald*, December 1, 1893, 8.

14. Julie Van Jardins, *Walter Camp: Football and the Modern Man* (New York: Oxford University Press, 2015), 92.

15. Jay Price, *Thanksgiving 1959* (Pennington, N.J.: Mountain Lion, 2009), 6.

16. Josh Tinley, "Football on Thanksgiving: A Brief but Comprehensive History," Midwest Sports Fans, November 23, 2011, http://www.midwestsportsfans.com/.

17. "Grange's Debut on Thanksgiving," Pro Football Hall of Fame, January 1, 2005, http://www.profootballhof.com/.

18. Rachel Bachman, "The Calorie Burn Before the Thanksgiving Festival," *Wall Street Journal*, November 17, 2014.

19. "Thanksgiving, 1896—Two Views of the Day: While a Multitude of Chicagoans Will Be Engrossed in Three Exciting Games, Others Will See That Charity Is Not Forgotten," *Chicago Tribune*, November 22, 1896, 41.

20. "Thanksgiving Day As Viewed by Seven Representative Chicagoans," *Chicago Tribune*, November 22, 1896, 42.

Chapter 7: Happy Franksgiving

1. United Press, "Thanksgiving Advanced by Roosevelt," *Washington Post*,

August 15, 1939.

2. Associated Press, "Roosevelt to Move Thanksgiving; Retailers For It, Plymouth Is Not," *New York Times*, August 15, 1939.

3. "Plymouth Pastor Assails Day Change," *New York Times*, August 21, 1939.

4. United Press, "Thanksgiving Advanced by Roosevelt."

5. Associated Press, "New Thanksgiving Date Won't Help Football Classics," *Hartford Courant*, August 15, 1939.

6. "The Year We Had Two Thanksgivings," Franklin D. Roosevelt Presidential Library and Museum, http://docs.fdrlibrary.marist.edu/thanksg.html#1.

7. "President Shocks Football Coaches," *New York Times*, August 16, 1939.

8. Ibid.

9. "Poultry Group Protests Thanksgiving Shift; Earlier Date Will Disrupt Frederick Holiday," *Washington Post*, August 17, 1939.

10. "Reaction of Governors to the Roosevelt Plan," *New York Times*, August 16, 1939.

11. "Shift in Thanksgiving Date Arouses the Whole Country," *New York Times*, August 16, 1939.

12. "Reaction of Governors to the Roosevelt Plan."

13. Ibid.

14. Ibid.

15. George Gallup, "The Gallup Poll: Thanksgiving Shift Seen through Party Glasses; Democrats For, G.O.P. Against," *Washington Post*, August 25, 1939.

16. "The Year We Had Two Thanksgivings."

17. Ibid.

18. Ibid.

19. Ibid.

20. Ibid.

21. Ibid.

22. "Poultry Group Protests Thanksgiving Shift."

23. "The Year We Had Two Thanksgivings."

24. "Early Thanksgiving Not Worth Extra Turkey or Doll," *Wall Street Journal*, March 15, 1941.

25. "Thanksgiving Goes Back to Old Date in '42; President Says Change Did Not Boom Trade," *New York Times*, May 21, 1941.

26. Mark Sullivan, "Thanksgiving Day," *Washington Post*, May 21, 1941.

27. "The Thanksgiving Before War, 1941," Franklin D. Roosevelt Presidential Library and Museum, Collections and Programs, https://fdrlibrary. wordpress.com/tag/thanksgiving/.

Chapter 8: Day of Mourning

1. Suzan Shown Harjo, a Cheyenne, as quoted in Peter S. Goodman, "For Native Americans, a Day of Mixed Emotions," *Washington Post*, November 26, 1998.

2. "Thanksgiving Day 2012," Letter to the tribal community from Cedric Cromwell, chairman and president of the Mashpee Wampanoag Tribe, posted on the tribal website's blog on November 22, 2012, http://www. mashpeewampanoagtribe.com/blog/?m=201211.

3. Edward Winslow, *Good Newes from New England: A True Relation of Things Very Remarkable at the Plantation of Plimoth in New England* (1624; Bedford, Mass.: Applewood Books, 1998), 37.

4. William Bradford, *Of Plymouth Plantation, 1620–1647*, ed. Samuel Eliot Morison (New York: Knopf, 2000), 114.

5. Dennis Zotigh, "Do American Indians Celebrate Thanksgiving?" National Museum of the American Indian, November 26, 2013, http://blog. nmai.si.edu/.

6. William Loren Katz, "The Politics of Thanksgiving Day," Zinn Education Project, November 26, 2014, http://www.zinnedproject.org.

7. For more information on the Pequot War, visit www.PequotWar.org, a project of the Mashantucket Pequot Museum and Research Center.

8. Benjamin Trumbull, *A Complete History of Connecticut, Civil and Ecclesiastical, from the Emigration of Its First Planters from England in 1630 to 1713* (Hartford: Hudson & Goodwin, 1797), vol. 1, 87.

9. Robert Jensen, "Why We Shouldn't Celebrate Thanksgiving," Alter-

Net, November 21, 2007, http://alternet.org/.

10. The "Suppressed Speech" of Wamsutta is available on the website of the United American Indians of New England, http://www.uaine.org.

11. Interview with Andrea Carmen, executive director, International Indian Treaty Council, January 2016.

Chapter 9: Helping Hands

1. Sarah Josepha Hale, "A New National Holiday," Editors' Table, *Godey's Lady's Book*, November 1870.

2. "Giving Thanks: The Religious Roots of Thanksgiving," Pilgrim Hall Museum, http://www.pilgrimhallmuseum.org/giving_thanks.htm.

3. "Boston, November 28," *Connecticut Courant*, December 1, 1766, 4.

4. Virginia T. Smith, "Thanksgiving and the Poor," Letter to the Editor, *Hartford Daily Courant*, November 23, 1882, 2.

5. "Roxy Croft," *Godey's Lady's Book*, May 1863, 437.

6. Gertrude Garrison, "How He Got In: A Thanksgiving Story of a Boy in Real Life," *Cambridge Chronicle* (Massachusetts), November 24, 1888.

7. O. Henry, "Two Thanksgiving Day Gentlemen," *The Trimmed Lamp and Other Stories of the Four Million* (New York: McClure, Phillips & Co., 1907), 50–58.

8. Karl Zinsmeister, *The Almanac of American Philanthropy* (Washington, D.C.: Philanthropy Roundtable, 2016), 166–67.

9. "Thanksgiving Day," *Evening Star* (Washington, D.C.), November 25, 1864.

10. Ron Chernow, *Washington: A Life* (New York: Penguin, 2011), as quoted in Zinsmeister, *Almanac of American Philanthropy*, 249.

11. Toni Myers, "Women Who Serve: Pastor Gretchen and the 'No-Cost' Thanksgiving Meal," Women's Voices for Change, November 25, 2015, http://www.womensvoicesforchange.org.

12. Patricia Yarberry Allen, "The New Thanksgiving: Memories of a Faithful Dog," Women's Voices for Change, November 29, 2015, http://www.womensvoicesforchange.org.

13. William McGurn, "Government vs. Soup Kitchen," *Wall Street Journal*, November 22, 2011.

14. Interview with Paul Shipman, marketing and communications director, Connecticut Food Bank, November 2015.

15. Joseph P. Barrett, "This Friday Was Black with Traffic," *Philadelphia Inquirer*, November 25, 1994.

16. Interview with Henry Timms, executive director, 92nd Street Y, New York City, January 2016.

Chapter 10: Turkey Day

1. This quotation may be apocryphal. The Museum of American Finance in New York City says that it cannot find the statement in Hamilton's papers.

2. "The Word on the Bird," *Consumer Reports,* November 2014, 23.

3. For a description of the foods that the Pilgrims and the Indians probably ate at the First Thanksgiving, see the Plimoth Plantation website, http://www.plimoth.org, especially the article "Partakers of Our Plenty: Thanksgiving Food Traditions."

4. Libby H. O'Connell, *The American Plate: A Culinary History in 100 Bites* (Naperville, Ill.: Sourcebooks, 2014), 4.

5. William DeLoss Love, *The Fast and Thanksgiving Days of New England* (Boston: Houghton, Mifflin & Co., 1895), 422 n.1

6. Andrew F. Smith, *The Turkey: An American Story* (Chicago: University of Illinois Press, 2006), 68.

7. Juliana Smith's account of her family's Thanksgiving dinner is found in a letter to "Dear Cousin Betsey" that she copied into her diary. It first appeared in print in Helen Evertson Smith, *Colonial Days and Ways, As Gathered from Family Papers* (New York: Ungar, 1900), 291–97.

8. "Thanksgiving Day," Letter to the Editor, *Norwich Weekly Register*, as reprinted in the *Connecticut Courant*, December 10, 1792.

9. Amelia Simmons, *American Cookery* (Hartford: Hudson & Goodwin, 1796), facsimile published as *The First American Cookbook* (New York: Dover Publications, 1958).

10. Sarah Josepha Hale, *Northwood: A Tale of New England*, 1st ed. (Boston: Bowles & Dearborn, 1827), vol. 1, 109.

11. Harriet Beecher Stowe, "How We Kept Thanksgiving at Oldtown," chap. 27 of *Oldtown Folks* (Boston: Fields, Osgood & Co., 1869).

12. Clementine Paddleford, *How America Eats* (New York: Charles Schribner's Sons, 1960), 21.

13. Ibid., 23.

14. Ibid., 20.

15. James Earl, Mary C. Kennamer, and Ron Brenneman, "History of the Wild Turkey in America," *National Wild Turkey Federation Bulletin*, no. 15.

16. Smith, *The Turkey: An American Story*, 59.

17. *Daily Tombstone* (Arizona), November 26, 1886.

18. Emma Paddock Telford, "The Thanksgiving Dinner," *San Francisco Call*, November 24, 1901, 17.

19. "Turkeys Sell as High as 40 Cents," *Star-Independent* (Harrisburg, Pa.), November 25, 1914.

20. Jennifer Giambrone, "White House Thanksgiving Turkeys in the Roaring '20s," The White House Historical Association, http://www.whitehousehistory.org.

21. Betty C. Monkman, "Pardoning the Thanksgiving Turkey," The White House Historical Association, http://www.whithousehistory.org.

22. *America's War on "Carcinogens": Reassessing the Use of Animal Tests to Predict Human Cancer Risks*, American Council on Science and Health, January 2005, 117–18.

23. "More Cranberries?" Caption to photograph in *New York Times*, November 27, 1959.

24. William Andrus Alcott, ed., *The Moral Reformer and Teacher on the Human Constitution*, vol. 1 (Boston: Light & Horton, 1835), 352–53.

25. "Thanksgiving Day," Letter to the Editor, *Connecticut Courant*.

26. Jonathan Lopez, "The American Character," *Wall Street Journal*, November 9–10, 2013, C5.

INDEX

A NOTE ON THE TYPE

The body of this book is composed in Hoefler Text, a family of old-style serif typefaces designed by Jonathan Hoefler in 1991. With Garamond and Janson in mind, he made this family specifically to fulfill the new demands presented by the digital era on the printed word—and the word on the screen—while staying true to the art of fine typography. It soon became a precedent for other typefaces to follow. The display text is set in its companion suite for larger sizes, Hoefler Titling. Together, Hoefler Text and Titling form a whole that is equally classic and modern, elegant and energetic.

The display text in "Readings for Thanksgiving Day" and "Thanksgiving Recipes and Bills of Fare" is set in Botanical Scribe, which was fashioned by Brian Willson in 2013. It is adapted from the cursive of the greatest of botanical illustrators, Pierre-Joseph Redouté (1759–1840), as it appeared on his stipple engravings of roses, lilies, and other garden delights. Botanical Scribe was chosen because its low-contrast line, following a precise and delicate geometry, harmonizes well with the line-dominated watercolors that adorn the text. Among fonts modeled on antique scripts, it is exceptionally legible. The signature of Abigail Adams is set in a font bearing her name and based on her very own handwriting. Though falling short of Redouté's exquisite letters in beauty and clarity, it is lively and sure. The Abigail Adams font was created by Willson in 2014.

DESIGN & COMPOSITION BY KATHERINE MESSENGER